D1442545

CALIFORNIA WILD

Preserving the Spirit and Beauty of Our Land

Text by Tim Palmer
Photography by Terry Donnelly, Mary Liz Austin,
and Tim Palmer
Foreword by Senator Barbara Boxer

Voyageur Press

Copyright © 2004 by Tim Palmer
Photographs © 2004 by Terry Donnelly, Mary Liz Austin, and Tim Palmer

All rights reserved. No part of this work may be reproduced or used in any form by any means—graphic, electronic, or mechanical, including photocopying, recording, taping, or any information storage and retrieval system—without written permission of the publisher.

Edited by Kari Cornell
Designed by Andrea Rud
Printed in China

04   05   06   07   08   5   4   3   2   1

Library of Congress Cataloging-in-Publication Data
Palmer, Tim, 1948–
   California wild : preserving the spirit and beauty of our land / text by Tim Palmer ; photography by Terry Donnelly, Mary Liz Austin, and Tim Palmer.
      p. cm.
   ISBN 0-89658-651-0 (hardcover)
   1. California—Pictorial works. 2. California—Description and travel. 3. Wilderness areas—California—Pictorial works. 4. Natural history—California—Pictorial works. 5. Landscape—California—Pictorial works. 6. California—Environmental conditions. I. Donnelly, Terry, 1949– II. Austin, Mary Liz. III. Title.
   F862.P27 2004
   917.9'4—dc22

                              2004002953

Distributed in Canada by Raincoast Books
9050 Shaughnessy Street, Vancouver, B.C. V6P 6E5

Published by Voyageur Press, Inc.
123 North Second Street, P.O. Box 338
Stillwater, MN 55082 U.S.A.
651-430-2210, fax 651-430-2211
books@voyageurpress.com
www.voyageurpress.com

Educators, fundraisers, premium and gift buyers, publicists, and marketing managers: Looking for creative products and new sales ideas? Voyageur Press books are available at special discounts when purchased in quantities, and special editions can be created to your specifications. For details contact the marketing department at 800-888-9653.

FRONT COVER PHOTOGRAPH YOSEMITE VALLEY © MARY LIZ AUSTIN
BACK COVER PHOTOGRAPHS, CLOCKWISE FROM UPPER LEFT:
© TERRY DONNELLY; © TERRY DONNELLY; © MARY LIZ AUSTIN;
© TIM PALMER

ON PAGE 1: Along the Pacific Ocean near Carmel, seaside daisies and other coastal plants bloom and unfurl new leaves at the continent's edge of rock and surf. PHOTOGRAPH BY MARY LIZ AUSTIN

ON PAGE 2: Half Dome soars up from Yosemite Valley, one of the premier natural wonders of the world. PHOTOGRAPH BY TERRY DONNELLY

ON PAGE 3: Sand verbena brightens the Anza-Borrego Desert beneath the sharp, earthquake-induced rise of the Santa Rosa Mountains. PHOTOGRAPH BY TERRY DONNELLY

ON PAGE 4: Coastal fog wafts to the uplands of Redwood National Park, bringing welcome moisture to bigleaf lupine and Oregon white oaks. PHOTOGRAPH BY TERRY DONNELLY

ON PAGE 5: Monterey cypress are at home in the salt air while annual grasses sprout with springtime green at Point Lobos State Reserve. PHOTOGRAPH BY TERRY DONNELLY

ON PAGE 6: In Death Valley—California's largest national park—morning sun reflects from the eroding facets of upthrust rocks at Aguereberry Point. PHOTOGRAPH BY TERRY DONNELLY

ON PAGE 7: Shifting sands at the Mesquite Flat Dunes create new patterns daily in the Mojave Desert near Stove Pipe Wells. The Grapevine Mountains rise in the distance. PHOTOGRAPH BY TERRY DONNELLY

ON PAGE 8: At Muir Woods National Monument just north of San Francisco, coast redwoods reach skyward in a magnificent grove named for America's pioneering protector of wildness, John Muir. PHOTOGRAPH BY TERRY DONNELLY

ON PAGE 10: The wildest large river on the West Coast south of Canada, the Klamath rushes past Portuguese Creek and powerfully cross-cuts its way through resistant rock of the Coast Ranges. PHOTOGRAPH BY TIM PALMER

ON THE TITLE PAGE: In the southern Sierra, a new day begins as early morning light reflects on the calm waters of Hitchcock Lakes, southwest of Mount Whitney. PHOTOGRAPH BY TIM PALMER

DEDICATION

These words and photographs are dedicated to all the people who have worked to protect wild places.

ACKNOWLEDGMENTS

Thanks, first of all, to my wife, Ann Vileisis, who has supported this book in many ways. Her contributions include a sharp and insightful edit of everything I wrote. Along with Ann, Jerry Meral of the Planning and Conservation League Foundation and Steve Evans of Friends of the River read the entire manuscript. Each applied a lifetime of knowledge about California in responding to what I wrote. Nat Hart reviewed the copy with the sharp eye of a veteran English professor and also the warm heart of a good friend.

At Voyageur Press, Michael Dregni launched this project with great vision and gave it the momentum that every book needs from an editor-in-chief. Professional in all ways, Kari Cornell followed up as project editor. Tracy Sheehan and Pamela Flick of Friends of the River and the California Wild Heritage Campaign provided me with reliable information about the current efforts to protect wilderness and wild and scenic rivers. It's always a pleasure to work with photographers as experienced and talented as Terry Donnelly and Mary Liz Austin.

Many people have inspired and helped me through the years. I will forever appreciate the lives, the work, and the friendship of these great Californians including Mark Dubois and Sharon Negri, Alexander Gaguine, Jerry Meral, Ernest Callenbach, Jim and Pat Compton, Catherine Fox, Yvon Chouinard, Grant Werschkull, Betsy Reifsnider, Ronnie James, and Steve Medley, to name just a few. Thanks, as well, to all who have come this way journalistically before me; see the bibliography for a short list of some of the finest and most informative writings about California.

—Tim Palmer

We would like to thank Tim Palmer for inviting us to join him on another collaborative project. We feel we are on the same page with Tim in so many ways and they are all good. And also thanks to Michael Dregni of Voyageur Press for his continued enthusiasm and support for our interpretation of the natural landscape.

Recognition is also due to our office staff: Ruth Anderson, Marie Harrington, and Margie Morgan. We owe them countless thanks for all the extra effort required at home while we are on the road.

—Terry Donnelly and Mary Liz Austin

CONTENTS

  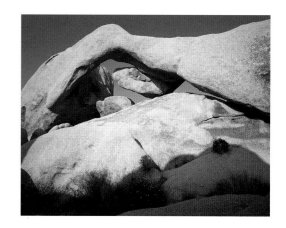

FOREWORD

by Senator Barbara Boxer

California's natural beauty has been widely acclaimed in prose and poetry. Our natural treasures have always drawn people to our state and been a source of pride and renewal for Californians. But that beauty must not be taken for granted.

During the past twenty years, 675,000 acres of unprotected wilderness lost their wilderness character due to activities such as logging and mining. As our population increases, development pressures increase. If we fail to act soon, our remaining unprotected wild lands and wild rivers will be gone.

That is why I have introduced the California Wild Heritage Act. This legislation designates more than 2.5 million acres of public lands as wilderness in eighty-one different areas and designates stretches of twenty-two rivers as wild, scenic or recreational throughout California. Every acre of wild land is a treasure, as the marvelous photographs in this book attest. The areas protected in this bill are some of California's most precious. In short, this bill preserves our most important lands, prevents pollution, and protects our drinking water supply and most-endangered wildlife.

This book, *California Wild*, movingly documents the natural beauty of California. May it inspire us all to work together to protect remaining wild lands before it is too late.

From its spring-fed sources near Mount Lassen, Hat Creek flows through wooded gorges on its way to the Sacramento River.
PHOTOGRAPH BY TIM PALMER

GOOD LAND AND THE ESSENCE OF LIFE

Everyone thinks they know California.

And they do.

It's sunny. It's golden and tan. It's trendy and casual but also strange and crowded. People think of San Francisco, Los Angeles, Disneyland, sandy beaches, redwoods, big agriculture, yellow smog, and much more. In fact, California is so big, so varied, and so complex that it's almost anything—you name it.

But before everything else that this place has become, it was a native landscape, shaped by primal forces of the earth and populated by animals and plants that belong in a choreography directed by the millennia. Fortunately, California remains a native landscape, including countrysides that lie either rock-solid or trembling under the force of earthquakes, along with water that pulses in rivers or foams ashore as the Pacific. It includes the atmosphere that whispers from above and sometimes storms down on us, fearsome but life-affirming. Altogether it's an extravagant place, incomparable on the face of the globe. And beyond everything that may seem typical or dominant, beyond everything that may seem passionately appealing or outrageously distasteful about the place and the culture, California is still wild.

I believe this wildness calls to each and every one of us.

We can see it in a translucent swell of surf at Point Conception or Cape Mendocino, in the vertical soar of granite at Yosemite, in the pellucid blue waters of Lake Tahoe, in the dazzling redrock cliffs at Joshua Tree, and in the comforting shade of valley oaks near Junipero Serra. Kings Canyon, San Gabriel, Sequoia, Anza-Borrego, Big Sur, Siskiyou—the list of remaining wild places tempts any lover of beauty and anyone who wants to know California as it always was.

Even with the changes that inevitably come when 37 million people—more than the rest of the West put together—set up housekeeping in one state, some of California resembles what it was when the first Europeans set foot on what should have been sacred ground. Since that time, much of the natural capital in soil, forests, water, and breathtaking beauty has been spent for the purposes of making money and accommodating human needs. But in spite of that, and in spite of the land that has been used recklessly in the process, a wildness worth saving remains. As a museum of past wonders, as a bank account for unforeseen expenditures, as a reservoir of hope for the future, and as a wellspring of life, the wildness of the land is now more valuable than ever. It's more precious today because it's more

Patches of fog drift past McClure's Beach on Point Reyes—a peninsula almost isolated from the
California mainland by the San Andreas Fault.
PHOTOGRAPH BY TERRY DONNELLY

scarce than it was just yesterday. Each day is like that. Each lends an ever-tightening sense of urgency to what might otherwise be a completely relaxed pause, here, in the comfort of beauty, in the satisfaction of solitude, in the heightened feelings of inspiration and perhaps even reverence that come from time spent with good land.

I get these feelings of inspiration and reverence when I stand at the edge of the ocean and breathe deeply the moist, clean, Pacific air that arrives from across the wilds of the sea. I feel it in the depths of the rainforest where the germination, growth, and blossoming of life inevitably give way to the death and decay that enable the coming generations to live. I feel it on the soaring heights of mountaintops that look out to so much other land, alongside the banks of a powerful river, and in the stark quiet of the desert, where silence carries a message of its own—one that can speak more clearly than the loudest voice.

In a conflicted, complicated, compromised world, wildness counts. It's important first because it's beautiful. That's the reason this book is mostly pictures; without needing words, the photos show that beauty satisfies in a deeply personal way and has value to the greater society. No one needs to apologize for valuing beauty over ugliness or over the mediocrity and the blandness that result from so much of what we do to the land—every place rendered down to marketplace functions like every place else. Beauty, I believe, is essential to healthy living, to community spirit, and to a positive view on life. As the great forester, ecologist, and philosopher Aldo Leopold wrote, "A thing is right when it tends to preserve the integrity, stability, and beauty of the biotic community. It is wrong when it tends otherwise."

If the emotions rising in response to scenes of unspoiled and beautiful earth don't cause people to feel attached to wild land, no amount of reasoning and logic is likely to help. But being the writer as well as one of the photographers of this book, I feel compelled to say a bit more about the value of wildness—to try to spell it out.

People need wild places. This is evident by how many of us visit parks, forests, deserts, canyons, and most of all, the edge of the sea. It's also evident in how troubled, bored, and difficult people can become when they never leave a place such as suburbia, the mall, the office, and even the house. Perhaps we need wild beauty as much as we need to be stimulated culturally by books and music, and nourished by friendships. By "wild," I mean places where nature still dominates. I don't mean we have to go to a forest primeval or an untracked desert, but just to the wildness that's close to home, to the refuge of a town park with its cottonwoods and singing birds, to the murmur of a nearby creek with its jumping fish, or maybe to the wildness of surf at a beach—anyplace where the forces of nature can be felt clearly, tingling all the senses, even within a city. For recreation, for escape from the stress of modern living, and for a place to

reset our expectations and our perspectives on life, nothing can quite substitute nature, especially nature that embodies a sense of the wild.

Beyond all this, in a completely practical vein, we depend on the diversity of life in the wild. Most medicines, historically, have come from herbs and other plants growing in nature. Half the pharmaceuticals on the market today come from plants. Think about the Pacific yew, which grows in the deep forests of northern California, and from which chemists derived taxol to treat breast cancer and to save the lives of many thousands of women. Additional miracle drugs will be found in the wild, but only if the wild continues to exist.

It's easy for us to think we can get by without wildness, but most of the community of life has no choice; unruined nature is essential to creatures great and small. In turn, we depend upon many of those creatures as much as we depend on the local grocery store for food or on the kitchen tap for water. The salmon we eat, for example, spawn in the wildness of rivers and creeks and are caught in the wildness of the sea. They are only able to thrive if the streams remain free-flowing and without dams, the waters clean, the spawning beds not clogged with mud that results from clear-cut logging, erosive farming, or land development on steep slopes and floodplains. One might argue that salmon can be raised in fish farms, just as cattle are relegated to feedlots, but domestically farmed fish need to be treated with antibiotics that pollute the water, give rise to ever-more-resistant bacteria, and find their way into our own bodies. Even worse, the fish from these farms infect the remaining wild fish with their epidemic-level of diseases, and they can weaken the native salmon's gene pool to the point that all salmon in the river could be affected. Finally, as any chef knows, fish-farmed salmon don't taste nearly as good as wild salmon do.

Consider another family of untamed creatures we need: insects. Without insects our agricultural crops would not be pollinated and, therefore, would not be grown, harvested, marketed to, or eaten by anybody. Many of these insects live in the wild, and if there are not adequate native plants to sustain healthy populations of them, farmers and the rest of us will suffer because the crops will not produce fruit, vegetables, or seeds.

Wine grapes worldwide are picked from vines grafted to disease-resistant roots that came from a native California grape. This wild stock literally saved the European wine industry a hundred years ago. Wild grapes, and any number of other wild plants, may be needed again for this kind of use.

People need hundreds of wild creatures, and all of them need wild land. Woodpeckers, for example, eat wood-boring insects that otherwise devastate forests. If we cut all the old trees—the kinds with dead tops and hollowed-out cavities—the colorful woodpeckers would have nowhere to nest, and would die or leave, leading to epidemics of wood-boring beetles and a loss of valuable forests.

These kinds of fascinating connections appear endlessly in the natural world. Wildness served as the wellspring of life since the earth began, and it remains the home of most creatures except us and our entourage of cats, dogs, cows, pigs, and the like. When wildness disappears, the habitat of entire communities suffers and the chain of life is broken with inevitable consequences, whether these consequences are felt immediately in our economy or felt only later.

Finally, the basic processes that keep life going depend on the wildness of nature—on nature as it has operated since the beginning of time. Here I'm not just talking about certain creatures, but about whole systems that maintain the earth in healthy and familiar ways. Nature reflects the working drawings for life on earth; it's the way things *function*.

Take something as simple as ocean beaches, one of the first landscapes people think about when you say "California." Beyond their central place in the cultural iconography of the state, beaches are important to people who like to walk there, to sunbathers, to surfers, to the economies of beach towns, and even more to a whole host of life in the ocean. But more fundamentally, beaches protect the rest of the land from the force of the sea; the sand breaks the power of the waves and the storms. Thus, beaches form our front line of defense against some of the most powerful and potentially hostile forces on earth. Anyone who has experienced a hurricane on the coast of Florida, or, for that matter, a big Hawaiian storm on the shores of California in an El Niño year knows what I mean. But where dams block coastal rivers, the flow of sand to nearby ocean beaches is reduced or halted. During winter storms, when beaches inevitably erode, there's no sand to take the place of what is lost, and beachfront houses collapse with splintered boards, bent rebar, and cracked foundations—the most noticeable of many troublesome effects when we upset the natural ebb and flow of beach sand.

Flooding rivers likewise replenish the soil of floodplains and recharge the groundwater that lies underneath, which in turn nourishes bottomland forests vital to 70 percent of bird and wildlife species. But when flood-control dams eliminate the occasional high water, whole systems of life collapse. The stream courses change and become less productive, and the groundwater dries up. The cottonwood forests die out, and when they do, they take with them many wildlife species—creatures that eat there, nest there, hunt there, hide there, or otherwise can't live without those trees.

Old-growth forests support a plethora of animal and plant species, help to control the climate, yield clean water supplies, and provide a refuge of genetic variety. Rare spotted owls and marbled murrelets need old-growth forests, and so do hundreds of other links in the food chain. When those forests are cut, entire communities of life go down with them, the cancer-healing Pacific yew included.

In short, wildness provides the underpinning of healthy ecosystems, and without these, both life and economy are diminished. Ultimately, functioning ecosystems are necessary for the economy to exist. At the bottom line, we protect wildness because it enriches us in many ways, economically, biologically, and personally.

Californians and Americans everywhere daily determine the fate of wild places that have served us so well. We will all decide what parts of this glorious but troubled state will remain with nature intact. We will do this through both political processes and personal choices.

Public officials with foresight have set aside some key wild areas as parks and reserves. Beyond those, a second type of wildness consists of extraordinary places that remain undeveloped but unprotected, their sizes constantly whittled down by new housing tracts, new shopping malls, and new clear-cuts. The natural world recedes in big steps with each 1 percent rise in the state's population. Finally, among the lands already settled or otherwise dedicated to commerce, wildness can be restored by setting aside small but critically positioned remnants or connective corridors vital to the greater chain of life. These might be swaths of open space that allow bighorn sheep to migrate from one high-country refuge to another, or sections of streams that link estuaries to headwaters where salmon, coming in from the ocean, need to spawn.

All three varieties of wildness—protected, unprotected, and restored—have made California the great place it is. They've served people well and enabled the larger systems of life to work. All three provide for the earth maintenance that gives us the soil we farm, the water we drink, the forests we harvest, the fish we catch, the air we breathe.

This book celebrates that wildness. The photographs show the real California that was here before any of us arrived and that must survive if life, as we know it, is to survive.

We'll begin our tour of California in the north, where Mount Shasta, within sight of Oregon, offers a sweeping view of its countryside—a place laced with wild rivers, shaded by coniferous forests, and mottled with hardened black lava that erupted from volcanic cones, fissures, and vents that plumb the molten interior of the earth. This region harbors an abundant diversity of life, and being less settled than other regions, it's a reservoir of wildness.

Then we'll turn south by following the coast from the redwoods of the Smith River basin to the Marin headlands, almost in San Francisco. Big trees, rocky outlooks, large rivers feeding the surf— how could anything be finer? Here at the edge of the continent, we encounter the limits of the land but the seemingly unlimited sphere of the sea—the infinite wild—and the view of that watery horizon can touch the spirit in ways that the view of land cannot.

Farther east, the Sierra Nevada forms a backbone at the mid latitudes of California—the highest, the wildest, and, one might say, the most geographically thrilling part of the state. This 400-mile-long range of granite and volcanic rock is so colossal and photogenic that we'll explore it in two chapters, covering the northern and southern halves. The northern half includes snowbound passes such as Donner and Carson, the sky-blue waters of Lake Tahoe, and Yosemite National Park. Perhaps no other place is enjoyed so thoroughly for recreation and escape. A southern block of the Sierra ascends from the giant Sequoias to Mount Whitney. For good reason John Muir called this the "Range of Light." Being higher, steeper, and more extreme than other mountains, it offers a wildness with incomparable opportunities for adventure.

Back to the Pacific again, and traveling southward, we find the elegant central coast, overwhelmed by the Santa Lucia Mountains and the magic of Big Sur but also variegated with related seismic ranges that sport oak savannas and poppy fields bright enough to dazzle the most jaded eyes. Linking America's second- and fourth-largest urban areas, and also linking the semiarid interior valleys of California with the Pacific edge, wildness here shows the value of connections: mountain to sea, forest to river, nature to city.

Beyond there, the mountains of southern California track southward in surprisingly remote ridgelines separating cities and arid valleys, some outposts still hiding from the glow of night lights. The fact that such island-like wildness exists so close to so many people is extraordinary in a world where such interplay is rare.

Finally, the desert with its quiet, haunting spaciousness reaches to Nevada, Arizona, and Mexico in a harsh but sublime elegance so different from the forests of fog-catching conifers and dew-dripping ferns where we began. In a world where noise so often prevails, the desert offers a soothing silence.

In the text that follows, I'll share some of what interests me and some of what comes from my heart when I explore on foot or sit quietly in each of these great places.

With these words and with photos taken by me and by the distinguished photographers, husband-and-wife team Terry Donnelly and Mary Liz Austin, I hope that everyone might come to better know the wildness that surrounds us. It still survives at the edges of a civilization that has often destroyed rather than sustained nature, leaving the fate of all things wild in doubt.

We have photographed without the use of distorting filters, without creating composite pictures, and without any computer-generated manipulation of the images. In other words, these pictures are honest. You can go and see what we saw. And you should, because pictures are only a substitute for real life.

Terry, Mary, and I created this book because the future of these places depends on people knowing about them and caring for them well. We hope these pages will provide a stepping-off place to really see what has always been waiting beyond the doorstep, whispering in our ears, calling out loud, promising the renewal of something special, something vital and irreplaceable, something that speaks to the essence of life.

Mount Shasta, the 14,162-foot strato-volcano in California's northeastern reaches,
glows at sunset above Casaval Ridge.
Photograph by Tim Palmer

Morning light illumines Jumbo Rocks at Joshua Tree National Park.
PHOTOGRAPH BY TERRY DONNELLY

Beavertail cactus thrive in the Anza-Borrego Desert State Park—
the largest in a magnificent system of state parks.
PHOTOGRAPH BY TERRY DONNELLY

CHAPTER 1

THE VIEW FROM SHASTA

Mountains and Rivers to the Sea

From the top of Mount Shasta, a thrill of rocky slopes and slippery snowbanks pitches down thousands of feet to forests, to rivers, to lower mountain ranges etched on the horizon, and to a distant civilization only vaguely indicated by the yellow-gray air it expels. I wanted to see what lay ahead in the course of the next few months on my pilgrimage to wildness in California, and I couldn't have come to a better place.

At 14,162 feet, this peak was once thought to be the highest in the United States. It rises with breathtaking symmetry from the lava plains around it. The altitude at the top of Shasta and the resulting thin air gave me a piercing headache, so I didn't stay on top for long.

Several thousand feet lower, I camped on Casaval Ridge. The snow had been melting for months and the once-velvety virgin surface now looked like the bottom of a million white egg boxes—a pattern called sun cupping. The gold of sunset still warmed the mountaintop, but then twilight dimmed on the summit and the sky darkened to a depthless navy blue. On a fell-field of volcanic rock, the moon rose big and round from behind Sargents Ridge. The snow refroze to an icy crust that reflected cool, colorless light while the rocks threw black shadows behind them in a starkness unknown in daytime. On this outpost nakedly exposed to the great climatic forces of the globe, the air—often stormy beyond belief at that high elevation—stood remarkably still.

With stars like fireworks frozen up above and the land like a dark mystery down below, the full effect of the view from Shasta now had time to sink in. Elegant in its simplicity, the cone-shaped monolith looks north to Oregon, only forty miles away, and east to Nevada, a hundred miles off. To the south, the Shasta foothills ramp down in big waves to the Central Valley.

Holding my attention the most because it embraced such a great expanse of wildness, the fabulous dark chaos of the Klamath Mountains jumbled up into the skyline west of Shasta, an empire of peaks and hidden canyons clothed in evergreen forests and severely trenched by a tumult of rivers crashing down like they couldn't wait to reach the sea. Fewer than five people per square mile live in the entire Klamath mountain region—less population density than in Montana or Idaho.

A geologic hybrid, the Klamath Mountains include subranges called the Siskiyou, Marble, Scott, and Salmon. The long, tapering expanse of the Yolla Bolly Mountains extends southward along the coastal chain and eventually merges with the hills of the wine country just north of San Francisco Bay, 220 miles from Shasta.

Snowcapped, Mount Shasta rises high over northern California. The dark lava of many volcanic eruptions has hardened into rocky outcrops.
PHOTOGRAPH BY TIM PALMER

In an amazing case of landscapes that move, the Klamath Mountains once clung to the northern Sierra but broke away and drifted seismically northwest, carrying native plantlife of the Sierra with them. The foxtail pine, for example, is found in these two ranges and nowhere else. Later, rafting in from the Pacific, smaller land masses called terranes collided with the edge of America to create today's coastal ranges. The total effect yields a continuous mass of rugged topography stretching from Shasta to the sea. With its geologic ancestry linked to the Sierra and its current marriage to the coastal mountains, the Klamath country features extreme gradient from summer snowfields down to sea level, most of which escaped glaciation during the ice ages. For all these reasons, an abundance of plant species have accumulated here. Thirty different conifers are found in the Klamath Mountains—more than anywhere else on earth. Two hundred and eighty plant species are endemic, a number exceeding that of every other region in America except the southern Appalachians. With such a remarkable tapestry of life, northern California ranks as one of the premier biological wonders of the world and showcases the value of wildness for the diversity of life it sustains.

Many of these endemic plants appear nondescript to the amateur botanist, but I wanted to search out one of the more spectacular specimens—the Brewer spruce. Though hunting for special trees had been a hobby of mine for years, I had never seen this rare conifer. A remnant from the days of colder climate, it can still be found on some of the exposed ridgelines in the Klamath Mountains.

After driving some miles on a dirt road, I got out and walked through groves of Douglas fir, mountain hemlock, and red fir. As I journeyed back into the mountains in search of this living relic from an earlier age, I felt like I was going back in time as well. Eventually I found a faint trail edged into the flanks of Sanger Peak. I scrambled up a rocky slope. Lodgepole pines grew crooked, blown into shrubby submission by heavy winds powered inland by storms coming from the world's largest ocean—silvery blue, far to the west. Reaching a ridgeline, I stepped up on a capstone of metamorphic rock and was overwhelmed at first by a vacuous drop-off into the Smith River canyon. But then I saw the Brewer spruce. Rooted into crevices, it grew remarkably straight, its needles sagging as if weighted by water. The limber branches also drooped, giving the spruce a weeping effect unlike any other conifer I'd seen in the wild. It had to be capably suited to the demanding geology and climate, yet the tree looked so delicate, so fanciful up there where ruggedness, even if concealed, had to be the byword for survival. A relic of the past, surviving the onslaught of countless storms and fires, the tree had also survived repeated phases of logging and mining.

Harboring Brewer spruce and other important groves of rare trees, some magnificent areas of public land have been protected as wilderness in northern California. This congressional designation bans logging, road building, dams, motorized vehicles, and development. Among the larger safeguarded areas, the crest of the Siskiyous runs south from Sanger Peak, the Marble Mountains rise in the Salmon River basin, the headwaters of the Eel flow from the Yolla Bolly–Middle Eel Wilderness, and the Trinity Alps cap the Salmon Range with the second-largest designated wilderness in California. Far to the east, the South Warner Wilderness belongs to the basin-and-range mountain region, more typical of Nevada than California.

Likewise, networks of five major waterways in northern California, including fifty-nine rivers and tributaries in all, have been enrolled in the National Wild and Scenic Rivers System—federal status that prevents dams from being built and that limits logging on federal land along the streams. This is the most concentrated region of protected rivers in America.

All the major rivers of the north provide a vital connection between mountains and sea. The Smith, beginning in southwestern Oregon and flowing into California, is the state's largest free-flowing river. Farther south, the Eel River and its forks drift past oak woodlands and some of the finest groves of inveterate redwoods.

With runoff from the snowy slopes of Mount Shasta, the Klamath River flows dam-free for nearly 200 miles across the mountains of northern California (five dams are located upstream near the Oregon-California border). The river transects the Cascade Range, then crosscuts the widest complex of America's Pacific coastal mountains. The Klamath offers the longest free-flowing and relatively natural section of river on the west coast south of Canada.

California's salmon and steelhead have spawned in all these streams. Emblematic of the health of our rivers and ocean, these fish depend on clean water, relatively undisturbed landscapes where silt and high water temperatures are minimized, and currents unchecked by dams. Once thought to be inexhaustible, the numbers of fish have been depleted and some populations eradicated. California coho salmon, which live in the rivers for two years before going out to sea, are especially vulnerable to watershed damage by logging and have been reduced from 500,000 fish a half century ago to less than 5,000 today, their demise sinking a $150 million per year fishing industry.

Klamath River salmon and steelhead once spawned in incredible numbers that fed the Yurok, Hoopa, and Karuk peoples who lived along the shores. Later this became one of America's greatest sport fisheries and supported a huge commercial fishing industry from Oregon to San Francisco. But diversions from the Trinity River to San Joaquin Valley farms robbed the Klamath's primary tributary of healthy flows. Ditches serving farms in southern Oregon likewise depleted the main stem of the river up near its source. The diversions caused water temperatures to climb to lethal levels and polluted the stream with mats of algae.

A history of misuse presents formidable challenges, but because of its remaining wildness, the Klamath illustrates the hopeful possibilities for land and river restoration. At relatively little cost, the third-largest river system on America's West Coast south of Alaska could be brought back to healthy status. The Central Valley Project Improvement Act of 1992 already requires that some flows from the heavily diverted Trinity be returned to the river, but lawsuits by Central Valley agribusiness prevent the law from working.

Recognizing all this potential but all these problems, I wanted to see the river top-to-bottom, so I decided to float with the current as far as I could go. Looking forward to several weeks of river-time, my wife, Ann, and I put our raft into the Klamath at the base of Iron Gate Dam, near the Oregon state line. Bound for the sea, we kicked off from shore.

On this watery tour of the northland we floated for days through deep pools and rocky rapids that quickened our pulse. We camped on gravel bars where the valley road had curved back away from the riverfront and left our site feeling as remote as Alaska. We hiked up the green-walled canyon of Ukonom Creek, where a waterfall burst over ledges and misted a whole Eden of ferns. We saw bears roaming the shores and dozens of ospreys soaring above the river, hunting for fish to feed their young. The relationships of predator and prey, parent and children, water and land were all evident in the graceful glide and artful dive of those birds, entertaining us mile after mile.

We portaged around a dangerous set of cascades that the Karuk had named Ishi Pishi Falls and finally drifted on the glassy smooth water of the lower river, gliding as quickly and inconspicuously as we could through the Yurok reservation. The heat of the interior yielded to the fog of the coast, chilling me in a welcome way and promising that the ocean lay not far off.

On the final morning, with the sound of surf signaling the end of the river, we let the current take us slowly out to a broad sandbar that forms in the summer and nearly isolates the Klamath from the Pacific. We beached there, walked across the bar to the breaking waves, and sat in the sand with a deep sense of satisfaction and with appreciation for what we had seen, all the continent behind us, all the ocean in front.

From Shastina—a volcanic summit adjoining the towering Shasta—the Cascade foothills tier down toward the Sacramento Valley while the top of Mount Lassen catches the light of sunrise in the background.

PHOTOGRAPH BY TIM PALMER

RIGHT:
Summertime snow lingers on the rock-strewn face of Shastina.
PHOTOGRAPH BY TIM PALMER

BELOW:
Hot days and intense, high-elevation sunshine cause sun cups and dendritic patterns of runoff to furrow the deep snowfields of Shasta.
PHOTOGRAPH BY TIM PALMER

FAR RIGHT:
Part of the Klamath Mountain complex, the Marble Mountains south of Etna Summit offer a resounding wildness of forest, rock, and snow. The rare Brewer spruce grows in cool pockets among other conifers including Douglas fir, white fir, and lodgepole pine.
PHOTOGRAPH BY TIM PALMER

FACING PAGE:
Magnificent groves of Shasta red fir are protected from logging in the Mount Shasta Wilderness, though unprotected land even within a few miles of the summit has been clear-cut.
PHOTOGRAPH BY TIM PALMER

LEFT:
From the summit of Sanger Peak, Haystack Peak rises to the west.
PHOTOGRAPH BY TIM PALMER

The Yolla Bolly Mountains extend south from the Klamath ranges here at the headwaters of the Middle Fork Eel River.
PHOTOGRAPH BY TIM PALMER

Deep pools of Ukonom Creek are crystal-clear in this undisturbed watershed—a sharp contrast to silt-filled streams that run through areas where many roads were built to serve heavy logging in the past.

PHOTOGRAPH BY TIM PALMER

Flowing through a wild gorge on its way to the Klamath River, Ukonom Creek provides cool water needed by salmon and steelhead downstream.

PHOTOGRAPH BY TIM PALMER

Ukonom Creek plunges over a waterfall in a remote and inaccessible corner of California's northern forest empire.

PHOTOGRAPH BY TIM PALMER

Carving through Oregon Hole Gorge along Highway 199, the Smith is California's largest free-flowing stream,
protected as a National Wild and Scenic River.
PHOTOGRAPH BY TIM PALMER

Though depleted in its upper basin by irrigation withdrawals and in lower reaches by diversions from its largest tributary, the Klamath River offers extraordinary potential for restoration as a salmon and steelhead habitat with wildness at its heart.

PHOTOGRAPH BY TIM PALMER

Grizzly Creek flows into the Van Duzen River, one of northern California's National Wild and Scenic Rivers protected with great foresight in 1981.

PHOTOGRAPH BY TIM PALMER

CHAPTER 2

THE NORTH COAST

Redwood Trees and the Infinite Wild

The summer fog throws down a blanket of gray, a watery atmosphere that reduces the world to two dimensions, lacking depth. The trees, rocks, and landforms look like cut-outs of dark gray pasted on top of medium gray, which lies on top of lighter gray until, in the distance, everything merges with sky-gray. But the fog eventually blows away or burns off, and then the California coast in summertime shines with blue skies overhead, brilliant.

Within this complex climatological process, sometimes cycling through daily, there is one supremely magical moment. Just before the gray turns to blue, when the sun first penetrates the fog, it shines as a star-burst of light, and yellow-white beams angle through the foliage from behind the trunks of the great trees. At that moment, on the cusp of fog and sun, the north coast woodlands come alive in unlimited glory.

Taller than any other trees on earth, the redwoods reach more than 365 feet. Among the world's longest lived trees, some endure 2,200 years. Their triumph of longevity owes to a number of adaptations to their surroundings. Shallow root systems, for example, take advantage of the plentiful fog. They can do this because the trees reach far into the sky where billions of needles intercept the passing fog droplets in sufficient quantities to cause them to drip down onto the ground. The moisture nourishes the shallow roots of the trees,

enabling the redwoods to cope with the dry months of May through October. The giant trees are also adapted to the dangers of fire; the bark lacks resin and fails to burn. Redwoods reach their greatest size along the region's rivers, and unlike other trees that die of suffocation when flood-borne silt piles up around their trunks, the redwoods simply send out a new crop of roots near the surface of the ground.

The trees are well adapted to all the hazards of their ecosystem, except for chainsaws. The handsome, soft wood—bug- and rot-resistant—is highly valued for siding, decking, and hot tubs. As a result, redwoods are among the most sought after trees for their lumber, and 96 percent of the old-growth forests have been cut down. Most of what loggers now harvest is second-growth. Parks and reserves protect half the remaining old trees, many of them bought by generous benefactors of the Save the Redwoods League and other organizations. The other half remains in private, mostly industrial forest ownership.

The 4 percent of ancient redwoods that survive provide an interesting perspective on the timelessness of nature compared to the suddenness of changes humans have caused in California. When one of these large trees sprouted, the Roman Empire did not yet exist. When Christ was born, the redwood had already grown for 200 years and was taller than any tree in eastern America. When Columbus sailed to the Caribbean, this tree had its 1,700th birthday and showed all

Dependent upon coastal fog for their water supply in the dry months of summer, coast redwoods shade an understory of sword ferns, salmonberry, and rhododendron at Del Norte Coast Redwoods State Park.
PHOTOGRAPH BY TERRY DONNELLY

the characteristics of an aged giant. At the time the California Gold Rush began, the tree looked virtually the same as it does today. Modern California, beginning with the post–World War II building boom, is just a blink of time in the life of this tree. Yet in the past century, we've changed much of the state so radically. Five million acres have been developed for housing and cities. More than a third of the land has been cleared for farming or grazing, and all but 10 percent of the forests have been cut at least once. Nearly every major river has been dammed and 90 percent of the wetlands drained or filled. Because the remaining redwoods survive from an earlier time, they can inspire people to keep some of that earlier, wilder legacy intact.

At Prairie Creek Redwoods State Park you can walk four miles through skyscraping groves the whole way out to the ocean. I did this one summer when the heat of the interior was blistering but the coastal temperatures hung in the damp sixties. It's one thing to step out of the car and see a few of the charismatic giants, but another to hike through them for hours on end, to actually sense that there's a whole forest of redwoods, a whole ecosystem of related life. At Prairie Creek, enough remains that one can begin to imagine what the complete forest of a century and a half ago—100 percent rather than today's 4 percent—must have looked like. Carrying my backpack, I wound through cathedral-like stands, up and down ravines that drain the deluge of winter rains, and out to the leading edge of forest. This is not a stand of redwoods but hoary Sitka spruce, which are better adapted to the wind of the Pacific front. They need plentiful doses of magnesium, delivered by the salt spray.

That evening, along the shore, I felt as though the age-old procession of life in California was reenacted for me. Thousands of pelicans winged their way north, returning to nighttime roosting rocks after fishing in the fertile upwelling waters to the south. Heermann's gulls, common terns, western grebes, Brandt's cormorants, harbor seals, and porpoises rounded out the scene. As the night descended, a racket continued from squalling murres and barking sea lions. This menagerie depends on a healthy sea and the intricate interface between land and water. The ocean has been over fished and damaged in many ways, but here one can still glimpse something of the original wealth.

Camping with a precious tract of redwoods not far behind me, I couldn't help but be impressed with the view to the Pacific out front. Absolutely untracked, uninhabited by people, and undeveloped, the ocean seemed to symbolize a wildness of the spirit—an infinite quality that can be felt in a humbling and even fearful way, but one that also offers the ultimate freedom of unlimited space. It goes forever, and I will never see what's there. All along the edge of California—even where it's urbanized—the ocean offers this unique form of wildness, appreciated by thousands of people who daily go to the shore to simply sit and look at the infinite wild.

The next morning, through the fog, which is denser than dry air and carries sound better, I listened to the bugling of Roosevelt elk—the largest subspecies of elk. Like the redwoods and other forms of life at the Pacific edge, they thrive on the mild, growth-inducing climate.

The fog again dissipated, and in the afternoon a steady wind out of the northwest blew shoreward, a powerful weather system that is typical of the summer months along much of the California coast. This is the famed Pacific High, a high pressure dome that governs the climate of the entire state and affects everything in its path—our daily temperature, the plants that grow, the crops that are raised, the snow covering the mountains, the fog shrouding the sea, the abundance or scarcity of fish swimming in the ocean—and so I was curious about how the Pacific High works.

The process begins far away, at the equator, where the hot tropical sun heats the air, which rises and drops torrential rains. Eventually the air climbs high enough that it cools, grows heavier again, and falls back to earth in two great belts both north and south of the equator. Cool, descending, dry air is what defines a high pressure system, and as this air drops down, the rotation and shape of the globe cause the wind to curve, relative to the earth's surface, in a clockwise direction. For the California coast, this means a nearly constant summer wind blowing out of the northwest, which guarantees the clear skies of summertime.

The fog we see on the north coast is intimately linked to these larger climatic forces. The northwestern winds blow consistently enough that they create an ocean current running from northwest to southeast. This brings cool water down from Canada, but more important, turbulence triggered by this California Current churns the ocean and turns over even colder water from deep in the sea—a phenomenon called upwelling. When the warm air of summertime hits that cold water, the air chills rapidly and loses its ability to hold water vapor, which condenses as fog that hangs in a broad belt over the ocean. When it blows ashore, the resulting fog-drip, caused by the tall trees raking this moisture from the summer sky, can total thirty inches of precipitation a year. That's double the rainfall of Los Angeles.

One of the persistent wonders of the natural world is that everything is connected. The redwoods need the fog-drip in order to survive summer drought. It's no coincidence that the redwood belt—400 miles from southern Oregon to the Big Sur coast—overlaps precisely with the fog belt, which in turn overlaps with the belt of ocean upwelling.

Wanting to see the wildest part of the entire California shore, Ann and I set out for the Lost Coast and Sinkyone Wilderness. South of the Mattole River, only one road reaches the Pacific in seventy miles. The northern half of this—along the King Range—sports long beaches where mountain slopes veer directly from high tide to the 4,097-foot summit of Kings Peak. While the climatic forces influencing California manifest themselves in the fog and the sunshine of the redwood belt, the geologic forces shaping the state are equally evident here.

The notorious San Andreas Fault lies just offshore. It marks the seam between the Pacific Plate and the North American Plate—two masses of the earth's crust that float on top a semi-liquid earthen core. The Pacific Plate slips northward relative to the North American Plate. During the San Francisco earthquake of 1906, the slippage between the two plates reached sixteen feet at Point Reyes, one of the more sizable jolts in history.

The San Andreas suture bends out to sea north of the Lost Coast, where the Gorda Plate crowds in between the Pacific and North American Plates with consequential effects of its own. This smaller plate migrates eastward, colliding directly with North America. Rocks that are less dense and thus floating on heavier substrate are scraped off the incoming plate and smeared against the continent, forming the coastal mountains of the north. Most of the Gorda Plate is subducted, or pushed underneath the western edge of the North American Plate.

Blocking the path of prevailing winds, the mountains force winter storms to rise up over them, and this, too, has enormous consequences. The mountains cause the air to cool and the rainfall to increase, which in turn waters the greatest temperate forest on earth—an ecoregion that begins with the redwoods in northern California and continues up the coast to Alaska. Precipitation increases by one inch for each fifty feet of rise of the coastal mountains; 200 inches of rain can hammer some of the peaks. In these ways, the forces of geology, climate, and biology relate intricately with one another, giving us the mosaic of life we know as California.

Walking through this area, we were constantly reminded of the weather that delivered the fog and rain, of the earthquakes that created the topography beneath our feet, and of all the spin-off effects that gave us the bugling elk, the sun-bathing seals, and the spawning salmon, which would enter the small streams and press up to the headwaters where they had been born.

South of the Lost Coast, extravagant scenery continues past the winsome town of Mendocino and on to the remarkable Point Reyes. Almost lopped off from the rest of the continent by the San Andreas Fault, this national seashore includes forests of Bishop pine, marshes with pulsing tides, cliffs that crumble into the sea, and miles of open beach awash in swells unhampered since their windy births off the coast of Alaska. The foresight of local conservationists in the 1960s saved the peninsula from a clutter of subdivisions.

Farther south in Marin County, conservationists also succeeded in setting aside the headlands north of San Francisco Bay as the Golden Gate National Recreation Area—a park unlike any other. Literally within sight of our fourth-largest metropolis, you can walk on trails to grassy summits that seem miles and years removed from the hum of urban California.

From Wolf Ridge, I gazed across the Marin hills to the shining white city that rises like a Mediterranean dream from the shores of the Bay. Because of open spaces such as these, San Francisco is America's premier city for wild country no more than a bus ride from home. My view also showed the chain of suburbs that sprawl east with little interruption the whole way to Sacramento. At the current rate of population growth, another half million acres—nineteen San Franciscos—will be converted from open space to suburban use in the Bay Area during the next thirty years. If protected, the wildness that now remains will be invaluable.

In my view from Wolf Ridge, Mount Diablo marked the high point in the coastal mountains east of the Bay. Beyond, the Central Valley sprawled with industrial agriculture and booming cities, but on the far side of the valley lay the foothills and the ascending slopes of the Sierra Nevada, where California's greatest wild country can still be found.

When the summer fog burns off late in the morning, the sun beams in white rays from behind the trunks of the redwoods. The flood of light silhouettes Pacific rhododendron below.
PHOTOGRAPH BY TIM PALMER

This majestic grove in Jedediah Smith Redwoods State Park is among only 4 percent of the original redwood acreage that remains uncut.
PHOTOGRAPH BY TERRY DONNELLY

Pacific rhododendron blossoms in late spring along the coast
of northern California.
PHOTOGRAPH BY MARY LIZ AUSTIN

An old-growth redwood grows upward toward the sunlight
along the Smith River.
PHOTOGRAPH BY TIM PALMER

One of the most accessible redwood groves, Muir Woods lies only a few miles north of the Golden Gate Bridge. Millions of people in the San Francisco Bay area visit the park each year.

PHOTOGRAPH BY TERRY DONNELLY

Home Creek rifles through Fern Canyon in Prairie Creek Redwoods State Park.

PHOTOGRAPH BY TIM PALMER

Deer fern, lady fern, and heal-all depend on fog-drip—water provided by the giant trees as their foliage intercepts summer fog and droplets fall from the trees, dampening the forest floor.
PHOTOGRAPH BY TIM PALMER

Red Clintonia is just one of hundreds of plants decorating the floor of an undisturbed, ancient forest in northern California.
PHOTOGRAPH BY TERRY DONNELLY

At the Shipman Creek beach on the Lost Coast, dawn illuminates a patch of Pacific fog. New wilderness protection is proposed near here on the slopes of the King Range.

PHOTOGRAPH BY TIM PALMER

Red alder trees, which enrich the soil by hosting microbes that draw nitrogen out of the atmosphere, crowd Low Gap Creek along the Sinkyone Coast.

PHOTOGRAPH BY TIM PALMER

FACING PAGE:
In the middle of March, Douglas iris make a floral display along the Sinkyone wilderness of the Lost Coast—the longest unroaded section of oceanfront in California.

PHOTOGRAPH BY TIM PALMER

RIGHT:
The Roosevelt elk, the largest subspecies of elk, graze at Prairie Creek Redwoods State Park.
PHOTOGRAPH BY TIM PALMER

BELOW:
Big seas pound the north coast where the collision of continental plates leaves rocky shorelines, craggy islands, and cliffs that drop abruptly into the Pacific.
PHOTOGRAPH BY TIM PALMER

FACING PAGE:
One of the favorite stops of travelers along the north coast, the headlands at Mendocino are a rocky masterpiece of scenery at the edge of town.
PHOTOGRAPH BY TERRY DONNELLY

Sandstone outcrops at Salt Point State Park result from enormous tectonic forces that
form the coastal mountains of the Pacific.
PHOTOGRAPH BY TERRY DONNELLY

Sandstone bluffs rise above the tide-line at Salt Point State Park.
PHOTOGRAPH BY TERRY DONNELLY

Rocky shores and tide pools invite exploration along much
of California's coast.
PHOTOGRAPH BY TERRY DONNELLY

FACING PAGE:
At Greenwood Cove, south of the Navarro River, sea stacks have been formed by surf-erosion that carves away soft rock and leaves the more resistant outcrops standing as islands.
PHOTOGRAPH BY MARY LIZ AUSTIN

LEFT:
Point Reyes encounters the open waters of the Pacific while evening light penetrates persistent fog.
PHOTOGRAPH BY TIM PALMER

The Golden Gate Bridge crosses from San Francisco to Marin County, where spectacular headlands have been protected in the Golden Gate National Recreation Area—one of the premier urban parks in America.
PHOTOGRAPH BY TERRY DONNELLY

CHAPTER 3

NORTHERN SIERRA

Forests, Rivers, and Snow

Unquestionably the largest mountain range in California, the Sierra Nevada rises as an unbroken realm of forest, rock, and snow for 400 miles. Never have I set out for these mountains without a tingling sense of anticipation. I always know that something special is up there awaiting me: a waterfall unseen from the roads and the trails, lupine or gentian in full bloom, the track of a wolverine, the distant boom of an avalanche. Who knows what it will be this time?

Turning inland from San Francisco Bay, I drove across the Central Valley and then up through mounded foothills cut here and there by rock-walled canyons. The temperature cooled, and soon gray pines began to appear, followed by the long-needled ponderosa. As soon as I saw those trees on the greening hills, I knew I was back in the Sierra.

Earthquakes have shaped the entire range; at well-defined fault lines the mountains are thrust up out of the ground on the east side of the Sierra. The western slope inclines more gently, the entire range shaped like an ocean wave approaching from the Pacific and about to break.

The crest of the Sierra runs southeast for half the length of California. Public land accounts for two-thirds of the area, most of it national forests. One-fifth of the range—3.5 million acres—is protected in nineteen designated wilderness areas. Much of this acreage lies in the gorgeous domain of rock at higher elevations and not nec-essarily where protection is most needed for the many life forms that make the Sierra their home.

The mountains gain elevation southward along the crest, each pass higher than the one before it, each major summit closer to the sky until all this heavenly ascent culminates at Mount Whitney. Yosemite National Park appears exactly halfway through the range, north to south. Dark volcanic rocks and forests cover much of the ground in the north; granite prevails more clearly in the south.

If anything dominates life in the Sierra as much as the stunning topography, it's the weather. The winter rainstorms of the California coast turn to snow as the clouds surge up the forested ramp of the mountains. By 4,000 feet, storms often hit the freezing point and snow begins to fall. Some of the deepest accumulations in America result, two, four, six feet at a time. A total of eighty-six feet fell in Donner Pass during the winter of 1982–83. Gravity constantly compacts the snow, temperate breaks between the storms warm it, and rain occasionally beats down, all serving to harden the once-airy depth of powder and transform it into a crusty cover extremely high in water content. By the end of winter, a consolidated pack of twelve feet is common at higher elevations, a snowy wonderland that persists until June and provides water for the people and farms down below.

Together, the geology and climate have produced some sensational landscapes here in the northern Sierra. Great coniferous forests—where they haven't been logged—cloak the mountain flanks

The smooth granite face of El Capitan rises above the Merced River in Yosemite National Park.
PHOTOGRAPH BY TERRY DONNELLY

and create habitat for the pine marten, the fur-bearing fisher, and a host of other wildlife including the supremely elusive wolverine. Lake Tahoe, America's second-deepest lake, sinks 1,680 feet to its graben bottom. This oval of blue holds more water than all the other lakes and reservoirs in California combined. South of Tahoe, Yosemite became America's first large park, with more than 38,000 acres set aside in 1864. Officials enlarged the park, eventually to 762,567 acres, and transferred its administration from the state to the federal government in 1890, making this our third national park. The Merced River gently winds through flowery meadows in Yosemite's glacier-carved valley, but abrupt granite walls reach up thousands of feet. Waterfalls plunge from top to bottom, virtually ringing the valley, making this a highlight of the national park system.

Yosemite has been rhapsodized, mythologized, and acclaimed by writers and photographers for decades, but you have to go there to truly comprehend the frequent allusions to paradise, to Eden, to perfection. To really understand it, you need to stand in a meadow in the center of the valley and feel small amid such grandeur. You need to feel the spray of water in your face as the streams break free from their gravely beds to be flung thousands of feet through misty air. Yosemite Falls drops a total of 2,425 feet in several linked plunges, the third-highest waterfall in the world. The scent of pine and the rushing sound of bubbling water there fill my head so that I don't think about anything, but simply lie on the rocks, looking up in awe and feeling both excited and peaceful, all at once.

Not only is the Sierra a majestic mountain range of waterfalls, high peaks, granite walls, wild rivers, and deep lingering snows, but it's amazingly accommodating to people who want to see the beauty, to walk or to ski, to venture out and wander among the peaks, to feel the nourishing power of nature. Even though major topographic breaks do not occur in the high country that forms the backbone of the range, paved roads cross the Sierra from Yosemite northward in eight passes. These make perfect jumping-off spots for anyone who wants to explore the high elevations. Inspiring the phrase, "gentle wilderness," the Sierra weather cannot be beaten for mountain country. With the lengthening days of springtime, the snow packs down and its surface evolves into "corn snow" that skiers love. Summer rains are usually limited to scattered afternoon thunderstorms. Autumn lingers late with aspen leaves trembling in gold, frost chilling the nights. Winter brings a fury of storms, but the sky often clears in between them and you can bask in sunshine. At high elevations, this is the long season—November through April—and so to truly know the Sierra means knowing it in winter.

With this in mind, I once set off south from Carson Pass with my backcountry skis and pack full of gear. I glided through forests of mountain hemlock and lodgepole pine, in and out of ravines smothered deep in snow, and across wind-crusted slopes that angled up toward the forbidding face of Round Top Peak. Though I felt alone, coyotes, snowshoe hares, and Douglas squirrels had crisscrossed everywhere in the woods; their tracks showed the record of the past week's activity. When threatening clouds built up in the west—layers and layers of gray compressing against the mountain barrier—I stopped for the night and dug a snow cave into the side of a drift that had formed in the lee of a great boulder. After an hour of shoveling I had a cocoon-like cavity seven feet long and four feet high—just enough to accommodate me and my equipment. I pulled my pack in through the opening, lit a candle, cooked dinner on my tiny stove, and quickly sank into my sleeping bag for warmth. Though the wind howled and moaned in the trees outside, my shelter was utterly quiet within, my candle flame flickering, the Sierra and its five-month accumulation of snow sheltering me like a womb in the stormy night.

In the morning I awoke to a foot of fresh snow, the trees newly covered, the tracks of all the other creatures deeply hidden. Under clearing skies I climbed a thousand feet to the rim of the Mokelumne canyon, where a dreamland of snow stretched off in every direction. Though each peak wore a uniform of white, I could see that the mountains had responded differently to the forces of the ages, each slope and summit like original artwork on the horizon. The dizzying depth of the canyon lay a long flight straight below me, forbidding in its steepness and in its avalanche-prone veneer of new snow, waiting to slide like flour on a baking sheet that's tilted up and up until gravity has its way.

After years of traveling in the northern Sierra, I picture it from a series of mountaintops, each offering a scene that's instructive about the makeup of the region. In the north, Castle Peak, with open bowls of snowfields that later riot in wildflowers, looms over Donner Pass. Here Gold Rush settlers struggled over the Sierra but Interstate 80 now allows an effortless crossing. Mount Tallac, reached by trails from the western shore of Lake Tahoe, offers an eyeful of that deep blue lake where Mark Twain described his rowboat excursions as "balloon voyages" because he could see the bottom so clearly. Farther south, at Ebbetts Pass, volcanic spires, bulbs, and columns ornament Reynolds Peak. California junipers cling to rocks, some of the trunks six feet in diameter but only twenty feet high, stretching the mind about what a tree can be. At Sonora Pass, Sonora Peak looks south to hundreds of summits, enough to stir the heart of any mountaineer. Finally, as the highest roaded corridor in the Sierra, Tioga Pass tops the mountains in the northern reaches of Yosemite. Mount Conness—a long and difficult day hike—offers a comprehensive view back to the northern Sierra.

The peaks of the Sierra are enough to draw anyone seeking the joy of mountains, but in many ways the rivers impress me every bit as much. The Feather begins this lineup with wild, difficult canyons in the north. Then come the more intimate, intricate rapids of the

Yuba, heavily mined during the Gold Rush but recovering today and spared from further damming by the dedicated people of the South Yuba River Citizens League. The South Fork of the American has the honor of being one of the most popular whitewater runs in America.

The Stanislaus, with three exquisite forks, foams off granite domes and through mid-elevation woodlands. The king of Sierra rivers, the Tuolumne heads in the northern reaches of Yosemite and tears through its own Grand Canyon of breathtaking rapids. Finally, the Merced River completes the northern Sierra roster, plunging over Nevada and Vernal Falls.

In many ways the environmental history of this region is the history of these rivers. At Hetch Hetchy, pioneering preservationist John Muir waged his most historic battle against the forces of change. This valley of the upper Tuolumne looked like a twin of Yosemite but was ultimately buried under a reservoir for San Francisco's water supply. Seventy years later, New Melones Dam on the Stanislaus became the most contested dam in American history, built only after a decade of opposition waged by Friends of the River. On the American River, the era of big dam building in our nation finally ended when an earthquake delayed construction of the 685-foot Auburn Dam, allowing time for river conservationists to muster their case for sparing this wild river.

Yet the struggles continue; virtually every resource of the Sierra is in danger. Even with the era of big dam construction behind us, rivers remain threatened. Dam boosters continually try to reincarnate the economically pitiful Auburn to reap increased subsidies. Taxpayers would relinquish a billion dollars to provide cheap water for farming and flood control for new developments on the floodplain, all of which can be delivered with less costly alternatives. And beyond the riverfronts, forests are threatened as well. Lumber companies have already cut three-quarters of the old growth. The resulting loss of habitat, erosion of soil, and subsidized elimination of beauty prompted the Sierra Nevada Ecosystem Project, an effort to look at the entire Sierra and at the consequences of use and abuse. New information arising out of this led the U.S. Forest Service to adopt a "Framework" plan that called for the elimination of logging of remaining large trees and for the protection of streamsides. The George W. Bush administration, however, replaced that plan with a policy that allowed three times the amount of logging and widespread new damage to the fragile forests.

Throughout the Sierra, the constant pressure of more and more people takes a toll. Yosemite becomes a weekend traffic jam, smoke filling the valley. Housing, tourist, and gambling development at Lake Tahoe stymie America's foremost effort by state governments to reduce pollution and save an outstanding body of water. With real estate pressure on both the California and Nevada sides of the lake, even the strongest efforts for water quality have been thwarted by the addition of more roads, more building lots, and more construction, all of which result in more silt. Unless corrected, this will cause the lake to gradually turn from the bluest blue to an algae-based green.

Facing the threats, citizen activism is alive in these mountains. People of many persuasions came together to form the Sierra Nevada Alliance, with better stewardship its goal. The Sierra Club works to implement a plan that would restore Yosemite Valley and free it as much as possible from the effects of crowding. Friends of the River, the Tuolumne River Preservation Trust, the Truckee River Watershed Council, and other local groups in every watershed work to save the best of their streams and to restore what has been lost.

John Muir began the American environmental movement here in the northern Sierra more than a hundred years ago, and now, as we enter the twenty-first century, the challenges of protecting this remarkable place are greater than ever. But if any mountain range has the ability to inspire people to care about the future of their land, this is it.

The second-deepest lake in the United States, Tahoe's incomparably blue waters are slowly becoming clouded with silt and algae due to land development and air pollution. The League to Save Lake Tahoe works to maintain the clarity of the water.
PHOTOGRAPH BY TIM PALMER

ABOVE:
With Half Dome in the background, the Merced River winds through Yosemite Valley, whitened by
a winter dusting of snow.
PHOTOGRAPH BY TIM PALMER

FACING PAGE:
The spray from Yosemite Falls—refreshing to anyone who walks near on hot summer days—turns
frigid in the winter, blanketing the rocks with crusty ice.
PHOTOGRAPH BY TIM PALMER

FAR LEFT:
Carved by glaciers, Yosemite Valley is guarded by the vertical soar of El Capitan. Cloud's Rest and Half Dome lie in the background.
PHOTOGRAPH BY MARY LIZ AUSTIN

LEFT:
Pure with snowmelt even in summer, the Tuolumne gathers tributaries in the Sierra's largest highcountry meadow before beginning its remarkable descent.
PHOTOGRAPH BY TIM PALMER

BELOW:
A highlight of California rivers, the Tuolumne forms in the backcountry of Yosemite National Park and creates its own Grand Canyon as it churns down through the Sierra Nevada.
PHOTOGRAPH BY TIM PALMER

ABOVE:
Large ponderosa pines such as this one in Yosemite Valley were once common through the Sierra's lower elevations, but because of fire suppression and widespread logging of big timber, thickets of smaller, highly flammable trees have taken their place.
PHOTOGRAPH BY TERRY DONNELLY

RIGHT:
Mule deer, common in the Sierra Nevada, forage in the mountains through summer and migrate to lower elevations of the foothills in the winter.
PHOTOGRAPH BY TIM PALMER

FAR RIGHT:
El Capitan looms over a forest of pine, cedar, and fir, with California black oaks sporting autumn foliage at the edge of valley meadows.
PHOTOGRAPH BY TERRY DONNELLY

Granite domes surround the blue waters of Tenaya Lake in Yosemite National Park.
PHOTOGRAPH BY TERRY DONNELLY

ABOVE:
With unusual calcium carbonate formations and critical habitat for migrating birds, Mono Lake, at the eastern
base of the Sierra, was depleted by diversions to Los Angeles. The lake has now been protected through action
by the Mono Lake Committee and other groups.
PHOTOGRAPH BY MARY LIZ AUSTIN

Rising over Carson Pass to its north and the Mokelumne River Canyon to its south, Round Top Peak endures
the full force of winter storms but shines in white radiance on sunny days in the Sierra.
PHOTOGRAPH BY TIM PALMER

Massive storms throughout the Sierra load fir and pine trees with heavy snow that later melts to feed rivers with springtime and summer flow—California's most important source of water for city and farm use.
PHOTOGRAPH BY TIM PALMER

The winter moon rises above volcanic crenelations of Castle Peak, just north of Donner Pass. The California Wild Heritage Act would protect this area as a wilderness.
PHOTOGRAPH BY TIM PALMER

ABOVE:
Bubbling through a springtime blizzard, a tributary of Pacific Creek drops toward the
wild canyon of the North Fork of the Mokelumne.
PHOTOGRAPH BY TIM PALMER

FACING PAGE:
Leavitt Creek pitches off the escarpment of the eastern Sierra—far steeper than the
west side because of earthquake activity.
PHOTOGRAPH BY TIM PALMER

FACING PAGE:
The North Fork Stanislaus River is proposed for protection as a National Wild and Scenic River, a designation that would prevent future dams or other harmful projects.
PHOTOGRAPH BY TIM PALMER

LEFT:
In this mirror-like pool at Camp Lotus, near Coloma, the South Fork of the American pauses before coursing down through its whitewater canyon.
PHOTOGRAPH BY TIM PALMER

Indian Rhubarb blooms directly in the channel of the Silver Fork, an exquisite South Fork American tributary that was spared from dams and diversions proposed in the 1980s.
PHOTOGRAPH BY TIM PALMER

CHAPTER 4

HIGH SIERRA

The Range of Light

In the southern Sierra, everything is more extreme. As in the rest of these mountains, forest, rock, and snow dominate, but here an unmistakable grandeur prevails. Although the coast redwoods grow taller, the giant Sequoias of the southern Sierra are the largest trees—the most massive organisms on earth. Peaks of the southern Sierra rise higher and rockier than in the north, creating places of incomparably severe beauty. The Sierra's granite batholith appears everywhere—whole mountains of white rock hewn by a supremely talented sculptor.

At 14,495 feet, Mount Whitney is our highest summit outside Alaska, but it's not alone. Thirteen peaks in the southern Sierra rise more than 13,000 feet above sea level, and 500 top 12,000 feet. The line of peaks that forms the mountain crest typically soars two miles directly above Owens Valley to the east. In the high country, you can backpack for days above timberline, where the stark mountain beauty is unequaled. Yet life, as well, abounds in the Sierra. A step-ladder effect from high elevation to low provides many niches of habitat, and these mountains adjoin not only the forest and chaparral of the western foothills but also the Great Basin and Mojave Deserts. Among California's 7,000 vascular plants, about half occur in the Sierra. Here, too, is the second-largest area without roads in the coterminous United States—2.8 million acres that span a 150-mile length of backcountry from Tioga Pass to Sherman Pass. In the lower forty-eight states, only central Idaho has a larger wilderness.

The giant Sequoia groves make an excellent place to start a tour of this region. I think of these trees as the ultimate expression of Sierra life. Their foot-thick plates of bark seem to glow with their own radiance in the warm Sierra light, the golden boles up to thirty-five feet in diameter, the crowns of scaly foliage disappearing into a violet-blue summer sky. A triumph of life, they live even longer than the coast redwoods. Like them, the Sequoias have resinless bark that's fireproof. Some continue growing for 3,500 years, getting thicker all the time. When lightening strikes other trees with ample resin, it runs down the trunk along the lines of highest moisture content, burning and splitting wood as it goes. But with the Sequoias, the lightening simply prunes off the top.

In 1890, Congress designated Sequoia as America's second national park, and then other stands of giant trees were set aside in Kings Canyon and Yosemite National Parks, in Calaveras Big Trees State Park, and in Forest Service reserves—seventy-five distinct groves in all. But in Sequoia National Forest, the logging of other conifers continued within some big-tree stands. To stop this, President Bill Clinton declared 328,000 acres of Sequoia Forest as a national monument, to be managed for the health of the giant trees. But in 2003, the Forest Service again proposed heavy logging of these same groves, which would leave the big trees isolated, prone to wind damage and overheating without the shade of the greater forest community. The forest battles of the Sierra continue, even here among the largest trees on earth.

Though heavily diverted, some sections of the Owens River still nourish a riparian community of
plantlife on the east side of the Sierra.
PHOTOGRAPH BY TIM PALMER

The Sequoias are not the only outstanding trees in the southern Sierra. Foxtail pines exude the same feeling of enduring life, surviving in harsh conditions of winter cold, summer drought, and high elevation. The bark is orange, the needles clustered like bottle brushes, the roots metabolizing water and minerals from what appears to be solid rock.

Even though it snows less in the southern Sierra than in the north, this is still a land of extraordinary rivers. The San Joaquin, Kings, Kaweah, and Kern bubble off the granite and into peerless canyons. The Kings descends for 11,259 vertical feet from alpine meadows to Pine Flat Reservoir—the greatest undammed vertical drop among all rivers in America. Wildflower gardens give way to granite staircases of rapids and canyons that deepen to 8,240 feet beneath the peaks, making the Kings the deepest canyon in the United States. Where the gradient eases a bit, the Kings offers popular whitewater for rafters and kayakers. In 1985, irrigators in the Central Valley proposed damming this section. The Committee to Save the Kings River, however, prevailed, and the stream was enrolled in the National Wild and Scenic Rivers System with a special management designation that prohibited the dam unless Congress approved.

From the Feather River to the Kings and the Kern, the Sierra's rivers and mountains lie within a day's drive of 40 million people, and the effects include more than the crowds seen at Sequoia National Park or Mammoth Mountain—America's most popular ski resort. From the highest outlooks on the crest you can see westward to a gray stratum of polluted air blanketing the San Joaquin Valley below. Ozone results from car exhaust, the burning of fossil fuels, and agricultural dust. High pollution levels are recorded through much of the Sierra, and 58 percent of the Jeffrey pines surveyed as far north as Yosemite showed ozone damage. Efforts to fight air pollution fail to keep up with population growth, and the southern Central Valley now ranks as one of the worst air basins in the nation, challenging Los Angeles.

Knowing all this but still knowing that the southern Sierra offered unparalleled opportunities for mountain adventure, Ann and I decided to see as much of the high country as we could on a twelve-day backpacking trip. South of Lone Pine we took the trail to Cottonwood Lakes, climbing all the time. Because higher elevations are colder, each 1,000 feet of rise was like traveling 300 miles north. For a week we wound our way among the peaks, swimming in frigid lakes on hot days, strolling to the summit of Mount Langley where we lay on our bellies looking 5,000 feet down rock-strewn ravines, swatting mosquitoes in the flowered meadows that enjoyed snowmelt all summer long, and chasing persistent bears away from our food at night.

Eventually we arrived at Wales Lake, an exposed gem of beauty located far above timberline. Mount Hale rose like a vertical tower above us, Mount Whitney slightly farther away. The glaciers had scratched the vast sheets of granite and dropped erratic boulders randomly on the ground. The place seemed to have been created only yesterday, and we felt privileged to arrive in the aftermath—in such a fresh, new, unsettled landscape, one that was still taking shape with the occasional clatter of rocks in steep ravines.

Clouds built up over Mount Tunnabora, sending us in retreat to lower ground in case lightening should come. But it didn't, and we climbed back up for the show of sunset, bright light along with stark shadows everywhere, ending when lavender flooded the sky. Then the stars shone so close, the night sky providing a backdrop to silhouettes of jagged peaks all around us.

We set our last two days aside to climb Whitney. Because thunderstorms had been hammering the top in the afternoons, we wanted to be off the summit before midday, so we hustled out of our camp along Whitney Creek at 4 A.M. For awhile only stars lit the sky. A golden sunrise soon warmed the granite peaks around us. Switchbacks took us to a pinnacle-studded ridge that ramped up to Whitney's summit. At ten o'clock we reached the top.

Processions of mountains led north to a spectacular collage of peaks in Sequoia and Kings Canyon National Parks. To the east, Owens Valley lay in miniature, and in the south, granite spires yielded to domes and flattops, then to lower ridges and canyons that veined down to the Kern River. Far in the distance, and out of sight even from Whitney, the Sierra ended at Tehachapi Pass, where the greatest granite batholith intersected with the Tehachapi Mountains and their contrary westward arc toward the California coast.

The Parker Group of Sequoias stand tall along the Crescent Meadow Road in Sequoia National Park.
PHOTOGRAPH BY TERRY DONNELLY

The giant Sequoias are the largest trees
on earth; this is the Oregon Tree in
the Grant Grove of Kings Canyon
National Park.

PHOTOGRAPH BY TERRY DONNELLY

FACING PAGE:
Sequoia trees grow with pines and firs in an intricate association near Redwood Saddle in Kings Canyon National Park; elimination of the trees around the Sequoias exposes the giant trees to damage from wind.
PHOTOGRAPH BY TIM PALMER

LEFT:
Cirrus clouds above an ancient foxtail pine foretell an approaching storm in the Nine Lakes Basin of Sequoia National Park.
PHOTOGRAPH BY TIM PALMER

The San Joaquin is one of fourteen major rivers that flow from the Sierra Nevada; here the South Fork streams past an aspen grove in the John Muir Wilderness.
PHOTOGRAPH BY TIM PALMER

One of the truly superlative rivers in America, the Kings cuts the deepest canyon of all, 8,240 feet beneath the peaks that rise from its banks. This is the South Fork below Boyden Cave.

PHOTOGRAPH BY TIM PALMER

Fin Dome is reflected in the mirror-blue waters of Rae Lakes along the Pacific Crest Trail in Kings Canyon National Park.

PHOTOGRAPH BY TIM PALMER

LEFT:
In 1987 much of the Kings was protected by National Wild and Scenic River designation, which halted plans for a dam that had threatened the river below this site at Horseshoe Bend. The California Wild Heritage Act proposes to expand the wild and scenic status to better protect the lower canyon of the river.
PHOTOGRAPH BY TIM PALMER

BELOW:
The moon rises over Moose Lake at the headwaters of the Kaweah River in Sequoia National Park.
PHOTOGRAPH BY TIM PALMER

Many aspens spread from the rootstocks of a single tree, creating distinct groves such as this one
along Rush Creek below Silver Lake.

PHOTOGRAPH BY TERRY DONNELLY

Black cottonwoods grace the banks of McGee Creek, flowing from the John Muir Wilderness east of
Lake Crowley. In the fall, cottonwood leaves swirl in the swift creek current.
PHOTOGRAPH BY TERRY DONNELLY

FACING PAGE:
Convict Lake, at the eastern base of
the Sierra, reflects the white wonders
of winter.
PHOTOGRAPH BY TIM PALMER

LEFT:
Springtime snowstorms bury the high
Sierra west of Big Pine.
PHOTOGRAPH BY TIM PALMER

Mount Whitney, rising two vertical
miles above the Owens Valley, is the
highest peak in the United States
outside Alaska.
PHOTOGRAPH BY TIM PALMER

CHAPTER 5

THE CENTRAL COAST

Critical Connections to the Wild

Along with a lot of other people, I flew from San Francisco to Los Angeles. I didn't expect this one-hour excursion between America's fourth- and second-largest urban areas to cross so much that was wild. But it did.

I had asked for a window seat, on the right side of the plane, ahead of the wing, and once seated, I got ready to see whatever I could, my road map unfolded on my lap. One of the first things I noticed was the San Andreas Fault, angling in from the sea near South San Francisco and trenching a valley now flooded by several reservoirs. Then I spotted the Santa Cruz Mountains and the largest tract of undeveloped forest between the two mega-cities. It had nearly all been logged after the earthquake of 1906, but much had regrown. I located the groves of Big Basin, California's first state park, which wore the redwood-country suit of somber green slopes and foggy valleys. Conifers looked like shaggy fur from that elevation. The Pacific shore appeared to be outlined with a white pencil.

Monterey Bay bulged in from the sea, indicator of an underwater canyon that drops 8,400 feet to one of the world's deepest marine chasms. Struggling for some conception of this, I tried to picture the massive landscape of Kings Canyon completely buried in saltwater and topped off with whitecaps.

While the land directly beneath me became arid and flat, with a grid of farms diverting irrigation water from the Salinas River, the highest range on California's coastal edge began to fill my view west. The Santa Lucia Mountains form the celebrated tilt of coastline along Big Sur, south of Monterey. Crowned by a peak called Junipero Serra, the topography showed a harsh scratchiness of chaparral, the sharp tops of the Ventana Double Cones, canyons that I surmised were choked with poison oak, and a large acreage recently burned but recovering in youthful green. Different from all the Californias I had visited so far, the scene made me want to explore on the ground, to see every peak and valley.

Soon the twin ridges of the Sierra Madre and San Rafael began to rise, and they merged in some serious topographic chaos at the evergreen summit of Big Pine Mountain, at 6,828 feet. Then the east-west oriented Santa Ynez Mountains blended into the Tehachapi. Finally, the Santa Monica Mountains made their elegant stand facing the Pacific at the urban front of Los Angeles.

Flying over this country made clear the connections between many things. The streams obviously began in high pockets of moisture and then dug deep canyon routes to the sea, linking mountaintops to surf. Forests intermingled with grasslands and

McWay Creek spills from its rocky perch into the Pacific at Julia Pfeiffer Burns State Park along the Big Sur coast.
PHOTOGRAPH BY MARY LIZ AUSTIN

brushy chaparral in a curvilinear mosaic—patterns caused by fires that had burned here and there, sometimes merging together but often spotted and surrounded by older green. The big connection—urban to wild—was obvious because I could see that this sweep of geography both links and separates the two great cities.

Looking at the physical connections on the ground below me, I reflected on the other linkages I had seen elsewhere in California—the relationships we all share with the climate, with geology, with forests, with water, and with all the greater community of life. While people sometimes get the notion that wilderness is separate from people and human lives, the associations that I had seen made the opposite seem far more true: we are bonded so indivisibly and in so many ways with what is wild, some of it as basic as the Pacific High weather system or plate tectonics.

To explore what I had seen from the air, I later set off to see the region on the ground, Junipero Serra on my mind. But nearing the base of that rounded mountain, I was halted by the Milpitas oaks. Once there, I just had to stay. The oaks grow in a savanna—a whimsically beautiful blend of grassland and large, scattered trees.

Wandering quietly among the oaks, I couldn't help feeling reverent about them. Four and five feet in diameter, they branch upward and outward with limbs as fat as entire trees elsewhere, the crowns doming high above, a hundred feet across.

Oaks are keystone species, meaning that many others depend on them. Deer, for example, eat acorns. One hundred kinds of birds rely on the oaks for food or shelter. The acorn woodpecker—black and white with a scalp of red—collects acorns and then inserts them in cavities it has pecked into tree trunks. The clever bird will return for meals in winter. Oak woodlands boast the largest diversity of wildlife among all the different plant communities in California.

These were valley oaks—the largest oak in the West. While conifers darken the state's higher mountains, sixteen species of oaks reign over the coastal hills, the Central Valley, and the Sierra foothills. They live in regions where cities grow the fastest, and because 80 percent of the savanna is on private land, the oak woodlands are threatened. In the past fifty years, people have cleared one to two million acres of oaklands. Another quarter million acres could be gone by 2010. And it's not just development that's eradicating the trees. The introduction of cattle to this landscape initiated a tragic chain of events that now prevents the valley oaks and the similar blue oaks from regenerating themselves. Cows eat and trample young trees, the cattle introduced exotic grasses that displaced native grasses that had formed the oaks' habitat, and the suppression of fires allowed a buildup of weeds and brush unconducive to oak reproduction. As a result, the idyllic scene at Milpitas shows many large oaks but few young ones. In addition, an exotic fungus called phytophthora spreads across the state causing "sudden oak death."

Oak enthusiasts are working on ecological solutions to the vexing problems, but for now it appears that the only way to see that the oak landscape of California will survive is by planting, fencing, and nursing saplings.

I strolled among the big trees at sunrise, the low light of springtime angling in to heat the rough bark, the birds fluttering in and out of the uppermost branches, the breeze whistling softly through the shelter that the trees provide. Then, finally, I set out for Junipero Serra's 5,868-foot summit.

The trail followed a creek and then climbed, promising an earnest workout before the morning was over. It mounted broad ridgelines and traversed sun-crisped slopes of ceonothus, manzanita, poison oak, and chamise—the classic California chaparral of brushy vegetation that blankets slopes prone to periodic rages of fire. Then the trail crossed to the northern aspect of the mountain and entered the realm of sugar pine—the tallest of all pines. Soon snow whitened the ground. At the top of Junipero Serra I could see north to the heights of the Diablo Range and to the silver sheen of Monterey Bay. To the southwest, Cone Peak rose 5,155 feet tall and only 3.4 miles from the ocean, our highest peak so close to the Pacific this side of Canada. To the southeast—ironically toward Los Angeles—all I could see was mountains, and as a wildlands enthusiast, I felt that I had discovered a whole new state. For years I had explored in northern California and in the Sierra, but here was another empire no less than 200 miles long, a place where nature seemed to hold sway. It was full, no doubt, with both hidden delights and hazards.

On the way down, walking quickly but quietly through a zone of heavy brush, my mind lapsed into that blissful neutral zone, conscious only of what lay immediately around me. And then I heard an almost imperceptible thud of paws striking the ground in rapid rhythm. Adrenaline spiked into my bloodstream immediately, and I looked quickly to my left to glimpse a tawny, muscular body bounding rapidly away through the thicket. It was a mountain lion.

Such wildness remains in the Santa Lucia, and the lion reminded me that wild places are *alive*.

The west side of the Santa Lucia is the famed coastline called Big Sur. Often considered the most photogenic oceanfront landscape in our country, the mountains there slant into the sea with little hesitation, unstable rock sliding as if it were simply dumped out of big slurry buckets during winter storms. Canyon mouths make diminutive bays. Four state parks and the Los Padres National Forest occupy much of the waterfront. Highway 1 clings to a tortured course over ridgelines, up narrow draws and around to ocean views, high on the crumbling slopes of the Santa Lucia and then back down again to places where you can step out of the car and wade into the thundering surf.

Throughout this region the California condor, with a ten-foot wingspan, once soared the skies but faced almost certain extinction in the 1980s. Remaining birds were captured and bred in zoos, and now the offspring have been reintroduced here in an effort to prevent this largest bird in North America from going extinct.

Another one of the great wildlife spectacles of the West Coast can be seen effortlessly along the ocean near Piedras Blancas, a point jutting seaward near San Simeon. Elephant seals are the largest seal, measuring up to twenty feet and weighing 8,000 pounds. Males sport a bulging proboscis and claim harems, guarding them with resonant grunts whose meaning cannot be mistaken. Vicious bites await anyone who threatens the alpha male. At the brink of extinction in 1892, only 100 elephant seals survived in Baja, the whole species a victim of market hunting because the seals' oil was considered superior to that of the sperm whale. Making a recovery under protective regulations, 3,000 swam ashore along the Pacific coast in 1971. For many years the only place to readily see the big marine mammals on the mainland was Año Nuevo State Park, north of Santa Cruz. But in 1992 a pup was born at Piedras Blancas, and now more than 1,700 are born there. In the spring the seals group in huge fleshy piles.

Congregating on the land, but living most of their lives in the sea, the seals are creatures of both, bridging those two great elements of California.

To get a feel for how the wildness at the southern end of this coastal region ties in with all that lies around it, I set out on my mountain bike for the San Rafael Mountains, three quarts of water in my panniers, my camera padded against the jolting of my tires. Beginning south of Zaca Peak, east of Los Olivos, I peddled up a dirt road, the surface quickly deteriorating to rock and cobbles. The chaparral became mixed with Coulter pine, then the uncommon big-cone Douglas fir. The ridge kept angling upward, the trail switchbacking higher to 3,000 feet at a National Forest wilderness boundary. Stashing the bike in the brush because it's not allowed in wilderness areas, I walked to a ridgeline running down from San Rafael Peak. An archipelago of mountains rose all around. I looked for condors and didn't see any. But what I did see, overtop the distant ridge of the Santa Ynez, were the Channel Islands. Those misted summits, surrounded by the Pacific, lured me on to the southernmost wilds of California.

Morning glory and poison oak climb a fence post near Plaskett Creek on the Big Sur Coast. Terraces formed by seismic uplift of the land are evident between the seashore and the mountain slopes.
PHOTOGRAPH BY TERRY DONNELLY

The surf has neatly sorted cobblestones by size at a rocky shoreline in Garrapata State Park, at the
northern end of the spectacular Big Sur coast.

PHOTOGRAPH BY TERRY DONNELLY

The surf sprays high at Sand Hill Cove in Point Lobos State Reserve.
PHOTOGRAPH BY MARY LIZ AUSTIN

Kelp has become entangled and washed ashore at Pfeiffer Beach.
PHOTOGRAPH BY TERRY DONNELLY

RIGHT:
Offshore fog begins to drift inland during sunset at Pfeiffer Beach.
PHOTOGRAPH BY TERRY DONNELLY

Elephant seals—some reaching twenty feet in length—come ashore in the winter at Año Nuevo State Reserve. These fabulous marine mammals were nearly driven to extinction but have recovered because of marine mammal protection laws.
PHOTOGRAPH BY TIM PALMER

ABOVE:
Even from the city of Santa Cruz, the wildness of the Pacific is evident with surf crashing ashore while the sun sets through thickening fog.
PHOTOGRAPH BY TIM PALMER

RIGHT:
Rising directly from the coast between Carmel and San Luis Obispo, the Santa Lucia Mountains form the steep backdrop to the Big Sur coast, seen here just south of Bixby Creek.
PHOTOGRAPH BY TIM PALMER

ABOVE:
The Nacimiento-Fergusson Road loops in and out of ravines as it climbs the Santa Lucia Mountains.
PHOTOGRAPH BY TIM PALMER

RIGHT:
Ocean fog drifts over the Los Osos Valley, which is greening up with springtime vigor beneath a high
lookout on Bishop Peak—a refuge of wildness at the urban edge of San Luis Obispo.
PHOTOGRAPH BY TIM PALMER

Valley oaks—three, four, and five feet in diameter—highlight one of the finest oak-and-grassland savannas at the Milpitas grove, just south of Junipero Serra Peak.
PHOTOGRAPH BY TIM PALMER

While the valley and blue oak survive in many areas such as the Milpitas grove, these two largest species of California oaks are seldom able to regenerate because of ecological damage to the lands where they live.
PHOTOGRAPH BY TIM PALMER

The view south from Ventana Double Cone features wild canyons and peaks of the Ventana
Wilderness, which was expanded when new areas were added for protection in 2002.

PHOTOGRAPH BY TIM PALMER

RIGHT:
Endangered and at the brink of extinction, the California condor is the largest bird in North America. Biologists are hopeful that condors reintroduced into the wild will start a viable new population.
PHOTOGRAPH BY ERWIN AND PEGGY BAUER

BELOW:
The San Rafael Mountains angle southeastward from Santa Maria.
PHOTOGRAPH BY TIM PALMER

Zaca Peak rises behind a tapestry of oak woodlands, Coulter pine, and chaparral
in the San Rafael Mountains.

PHOTOGRAPH BY TIM PALMER

CHAPTER 6

SOUTHERN MOUNTAINS

Islands of Wildness

Southern California is ribbed and backboned by mountain ranges still wild at their core. The Santa Monica, San Gabriel, San Bernardino, San Jacinto, Santa Ana, Palomar, Laguna, and Cuyamaca are all high-ridged results of earthquakes that build mountains up and mudslides that tear them down. Wildfires periodically torch the incendiary chaparral. In all of America, there is nothing quite like the wildness found here: higher whisperings of pine and fir offer cool relief and collect drifts of snow within sight of a semitropical coastline or a desert far below.

These mountain ranges resemble islands in two respects. First, each has been surrounded since time immemorial by desert or dry country, which tends to isolate each landmass and cause biological specialties to evolve, though some more-mobile creatures overcame this isolation by passing from range to range along connecting paths that nature had always provided. Second, many of the ranges are now surrounded or bordered by suburbanization, and this diminishes native life by hemming in creatures such as the mountain lion and bighorn sheep.

It always amazes me that wildness survives so close to downtown and the plague of urban sprawl. Steep mountains seem to hang suspended behind every urban scene, assuming the air is clear enough to see through the intervening mileage. But unlike the fake backdrops used in the movie industry headquartered here, these scenes are real, and the forces of nature do real things. Earthquakes, floods, mudslides, and fires all reshape the land and rake the rubble into new shapes, and it doesn't much matter what is in the way.

A showcase of the south, the Santa Monica Mountains rise from the streets of the city, the ocean on one side of the range, the Los Angeles fringe on the other. Along with the Santa Ynez lying to the north, these are part of the Transverse Ranges, a composite of five mountain chains that align east-west on the northern border of the Los Angeles area.

Hundreds of miles of trails wind through the Santa Monicas, and to get the flavor for the wilder end of the range, I walked up Big Sycamore Canyon from the beach near Point Mugu. The deep boom of surf as well as the clatter of traffic on the Pacific Coast Highway

With canyons, mountain ridges, and smaller pockets of
wildness remaining, the Santa Monica Mountains rise from the Los Angeles urban area.
PHOTOGRAPH BY TIM PALMER

diminished as soon as I rounded the first bend in the path; the mountains already sequestered me away in another place and time. Chaparral-covered hills, steep and forbidding, could only be climbed by trail, the brush was so thick. The stream gurgled down from many tributaries but it lacked runoff from winter storms, so I could still step across it. On the floodplain, and stealing the show in that canyon, magnificent western sycamores grew broad and tall. Fat trunks wrestled their way not only upward but outward with unexpected twists and turns reflecting the stresses of circumstance and the opportunities of many years. Trees had fattened to two feet in diameter with stout limbs, some nearly horizontal and begging to be walked on or sat upon. As tree biographer Donald Culross Peattie wrote, the sycamore "cannot help falling into picturesque attitudes."

Unlike any other tree, these sycamores have bark mottled in white, gray, tan, pale green, and brown, each tone like a piece of jigsaw puzzle fitted neatly in or around the others. The big trees defy the dry nature of those mountains by tapping the moisture carried from summit to bottomland by the stream, and as a result, the sycamores tower over all the other plants around them.

I looped westward from Sycamore Canyon to a high point with one view to the Pacific, another to the ridge-and-canyon excellence of the western Santa Monicas, and yet another to the urban hum of Oxnard, all reminding me that the mountains here in southern California have remarkably different run-outs depending on which way you go.

At their western end, the Santa Monicas dip decisively into the sea but then reemerge as the Northern Channel Islands, a national park. Ranging between twelve and seventy miles offshore, five isles arise like shimmering mirages floating on liquid silver. Sometimes called the American Galapagos, these islands are home to eight hundred species of plants and animals, fifty-four of them found here and nowhere else.

East of the Santa Monicas, the San Gabriel Mountains form another part of the Transverse Ranges and create a formidable northern wall to LA's urban area. After a few dozen elbow bends in the road climbing this range, the chaparral begins to thin out and the ponderosa pines should be taking over. However, these slopes receive the brunt of LA's notorious smog, and most of the pines have been killed by the pollution. In spite of progressive advances and a reduction of per capita emissions, there are far more people now, and they drive far more cars than they did even a few years ago, and so the metro area still has the worst air in the nation. New pines in the lower San Gabriel struggled for life; I couldn't tell whether they would make it or not. After another thousand feet of climbing, I suddenly burst out of the inversion layer like a jet gaining cruising altitude above the clouds, the sky suddenly blue, the yellow-gray soup of lower atmosphere trapped by the cool marine air that drifts in

overtop. The roof of the smog layer now looked like the sea itself, as if the ocean had risen a thousand feet and flooded everything on the flats and foothills.

Up there with a cleaner atmosphere to breathe, California red oaks leafed out nicely, and then I entered a belt of surviving incense cedar and white fir. At the highest reaches, limber pine darkened slopes that pitched down the other side to the arid expanse of the Mojave Desert, a surprise of brown monochrome even though I knew to expect it.

The San Bernardino Mountains adjoin the San Gabriel and rise even higher. At 11,502 feet, San Gorgonio is the highest peak in southern California and creates some of the greatest vertical relief in America. Though Mount Whitney is taller, it soars up from a valley that's already 4,000 feet above sea level, and so the relative rise of San Gorgonio is about the same.

The extraordinary height of these two mountains is caused by a kink in the San Andreas Fault. Trending mostly in a straight line, southeast to northwest, the fault takes a turn to the west at the San Bernardino–San Gorgonio interface. As a result, the Pacific Plate here doesn't slip alongside but plows more directly into the continental plate, causing a colossal wreckage of rock that has nowhere to go but up.

Equally awesome as a force to avoid, fire burns here in an endless cycle. The chaparral that covers the slopes and fills the canyons ignites readily—almost explosively. Indeed, it was *made* to burn; in this dry climate, only fire can break down the biological products of dead wood, which is constantly being generated. Fires have always returned here in natural cycles occurring about once every thirty years. Massive mudslides then follow in the wake of the blazes. But now people incur enormous risks and costs because so much development has been built directly in harm's way—point-blank to danger in the fire and mudslide zones. In 2003, three-quarters of a million acres burned, destroying 3,640 homes built on mountain slopes well-known to be incendiary. Fatal mudslides came just two months later.

South of the San Bernardinos, the Peninsular Ranges angle directly toward Mexico and ultimately become the Baja Peninsula. Northernmost in this chain are the San Jacinto and the Santa Ana Mountains. With housing developments spreading throughout these and all the other foothills, the greater Los Angeles area has the longest urban-wildland interface of any non-tropical city in the world— 680 miles. Each day, as more flat land and foothills are built upon, more and more development comes in contact with the wild fringe that surrounds the LA basin. At risk, if not already obliterated, are the attenuating corridors of habitat that connect refuges of protected land in the mountains.

Wildlife, however, need open-space corridors to travel from one refuge to another in order to freshen their gene pool and to avoid the mutant problems of inbreeding, which can otherwise plague enclosed communities. Biologist Paul Brier predicted that the lions of the Santa Ana will soon go extinct unless we establish some protected corridors to the south. Facing similar problems, bighorn sheep have been reduced from 1,200 ranging the high country between Los Angeles and Mexico in 1978 to 475 in 2002. Interstate 10 has boldly severed linkages to the San Bernardinos and points north. Passageways connecting the Santa Anas with adjacent wildlands to the south have been reduced to the thinnest of threads such as a golf course and a freeway underpass, but even there, corridors can still be protected through open space acquisition. It's not yet too late.

From the top of the Santa Anas I faced the ocean of development leading out to the real ocean below. Off to the east, blocked from my view by other mountains, lay a wholly different landscape. Out there beyond the reach of the Pacific Ocean's moisture, the desert spread across the starkest expanse of California wild.

Poppies and lupine riot in dazzling color at the Antelope Valley California Poppy State Reserve, just northeast of the San Gabriel Mountains.
PHOTOGRAPH BY TERRY DONNELLY

FACING PAGE:
Free-flowing streams are rare in this region, but with runoff from the Santa Ynez Mountains, Santa Paula Creek pulses out from its wild canyon.
PHOTOGRAPH BY TIM PALMER

LEFT:
The ultimate predator, mountain lions depend on deer for a food supply. The mountain lion's habitat is rapidly diminishing because of suburban growth and second-home development.
PHOTOGRAPH BY ERWIN AND PEGGY BAUER

BELOW:
Annual grasses are ruffled by high winds on the slopes of the Santa Ynez Mountains, rising directly from the Pacific at Gaviota.
PHOTOGRAPH BY TIM PALMER

ABOVE, BOTH PHOTOS:
California sycamores spread their limbs in all directions at Point Mugu State Park near the
western end of the Santa Monica Mountains.

PHOTOGRAPHS BY TIM PALMER

Beyond a foreground of yucca, Mendanhall Ridge rises in the San Gabriel Mountains, a vast collage of peaks
and canyons literally at the edge of the Los Angeles urban area.
PHOTOGRAPH BY TIM PALMER

Lyons Peak rises to the southwest of Lawson Peak's granite summit, covered with manzanita, east of San Diego.
PHOTOGRAPH BY TIM PALMER

RIGHT:
Scorched in the fires of 2003, the Santa Susana Mountains north of Simi Valley were already recovering with green just six months later. This area of Browns Canyon was added to the regional parks system in 2003.
PHOTOGRAPH BY TIM PALMER

FACING PAGE:
Tranquil in its canyon fastness, Malibu Creek reflects the resistant rocks of the Santa Monica Mountains. To restore salmon and steelhead to this stream, Friends of the River proposes removal of an obsolete dam located downstream.
PHOTOGRAPH BY TIM PALMER

California sycamores tap the moisture of valley bottomlands at Malibu Creek State Park.
PHOTOGRAPH BY TIM PALMER

The uncommon Engelmann oak survives with native bunchgrasses in a luxuriant savanna at the Santa Rosa Plateau Ecological Reserve, managed by The Nature Conservancy and Riverside County.
PHOTOGRAPH BY TIM PALMER

Partly burned by the great fires of 2003, this interior live oak survives at the base of El Cajon Mountain east of San Diego.
PHOTOGRAPH BY TIM PALMER

Torrey pines grow only on Santa Rosa Island and here at the Torrey Pines State Reserve near San Diego.
PHOTOGRAPH BY TIM PALMER

CHAPTER 7

THE CALIFORNIA DESERT

Extravagance and Scarcity

Far to the north, in February, Mount Shasta rises as snowy as one can imagine. At its base, the rainforests take over, blanketing the mountains down to high tide line at the Pacific. The oak savannas of the interior sprout green and lush about this time, and the Sierra lies buried by blizzards with a snowpack that will feed rushing rivers all summer long. California has shown us everything—a geographic, climatic, and biological exhibit bigger than life—and now, to make the claim unequivocal, we come to the desert.

A large part of California is arid—acreage as vast as the forest lands of the north, as extensive as the entire Sierra. Roughly a quarter of the state, mostly in its southeastern quadrant, receives less than ten inches of rain per year—less than 10 percent of what falls at the Mattole River headwaters on the north coast. In some years, part of the desert gets absolutely no moisture, and all the while the sun pounds powerfully enough to evaporate ten feet off the top of any lake or reservoir that could conceivably be there. Though daunted by the lack of water, I was excited to see this harsh land and the resounding wildness that remains in immense dry spaces.

Deserts form for two reasons. First, in the Coast Range we saw that mountains cause the moist Pacific air to rise and cool until the moisture is released from the clouds in the form of rain or snow. But that's not the whole story. On the opposite side of the mountains—the downwind side—the descending air has not only spent its moisture, but it again warms up and surpasses the dew point, which allows the remaining moisture to stay vaporized. The combined effect produces a "rain shadow" of aridity. Being especially high and continuous, and aligned at a right angle to storms approaching from the west, the Sierra Nevada produces not just any rain shadow, but an extreme one. The desert begins literally at the base of the peaks.

The second reason for deserts occurs not at the scale of mountain ranges, large as they are, but rather at the scale of the globe. The critical interplay of forces is the same one that produced the Pacific high pressure system: the heated air at the tropics rises, cools, and falls back to earth in two broad belts both north and south of the equator. Where this super-dried air descends in the most extreme way—high pressure zones beginning at the fifteen-degree latitude lines both north and south of the equator—the world's great deserts result. This accounts for much of the aridity of southern California.

While aridity defines the desert, there's a surprising mix of life there. In fact, botanists describe not one desert in California but three, their distinctive plantlife a function of nuances in the climate. The Great Basin lies in the rain shadow of the Sierra Nevada; sign-

At Death Valley National Park, shifting sand near Stove Pipe Wells ripples on dunes while the
Grapevine Mountains rise in the distance.
PHOTOGRAPH BY TERRY DONNELLY

posts here are sagebrush, bitterbrush, and rabbitbrush. Warmer, the Mojave Desert appears to the south. Creosote bush grows here, along with the showy flourish of Joshua trees. To the far southwest, the Sonoran Desert's signature is the saguaro cactus, its tall trunk and uplifted arms an icon of old western movies. With rainy seasons in both winter and summer, the Sonoran has the most varied plantlife of any desert in the world—2,500 species. Six kinds of rattlesnakes can be found.

My first experience in the California desert came with a visit to Death Valley in the fall. This place is the hottest, driest, and lowest in America, and outside Alaska it's also our largest national park, measuring fifty by two hundred miles. Even in November, daytime temperatures climb into the nineties. Nighttime lows dropped below freezing at high elevations. I wandered down a dry wash from Zabriskie Point, with only one quart of water in my pack. The main channel—a bone-dry river of cobblestones and sand—grew from tributaries left and right, and at each juncture I wondered how I would find my way back up the correct path. Already down to half a quart of water, and fearing the cold of an autumn night in that severe, untempered place, I began marking my route at each look-alike confluence by placing a small stone in my path. The common securities that come with water, shade, and knowing where one is on earth cannot be taken for granted here, and that was my first lesson of the desert.

Astonishing features and phenomena abound: the extremes of temperature, the starkness of rock, the blue of vaporless skies, the flaming red of sunset. The spareness of life can shock a person more accustomed to forests or grasslands, yet the life of the desert is remarkable, hundreds of species fitting into isolated niches of moisture, shade, or shelter. Consider the fringe-toed lizard, found near the booming city of Palm Springs. This eight-inch reptile exists entirely in windblown sand, where it literally swims underground to escape 180-degree temperatures on the surface and to evade predators. Its streamlined jaw cuts the path it follows. Adapted nostrils allow it to breathe from the diminutive pockets of air between grains of sand. Eyelids overlap for obvious reasons, and a "third eye" lies on top of its head, sensitive to light, sound, and vibrations, including those that indicate insects—the lizard's prey. Because golf courses and urban development have preempted so much of its territory, this singular animal is classified as threatened under the Endangered Species Act. Many people have worked to protect its remaining habitat.

Silence is perhaps the most awesome of all sensations that press upon you in the desert. Miles of open landscape lie within view, and in all that distance there may not be the slightest sound—not even a bird on wing or a bug in the air. The magnitude of such silence can at first feel eerie. Then it begins to feel peaceful. Then normal. Then necessary.

Mountains dominate in the desert, just as they do across most of California. But lacking trees for cover, the gradient here is nakedly evident. In Death Valley, at the lowest point in the United States, 282 feet below sea level, one can eye Telescope Peak, 11,331 feet above. Nothing blocks the view or muffles the extremes of rise and fall.

A capstone to desert gradient, the White Mountains guard the northern end of California's arid empire. Almost as tall as the Sierra Nevada, which lies directly west, they climb 9,700 feet across only seven miles of pine-dotted slopes that reach to bold swaths of open ridgelines. The largest undesignated wilderness in California, 379,000 acres remains roadless here. This is the stronghold of the bristlecone pine, the oldest tree in the world. Some have been living more than 5,000 years, short and gnarled, weathered by the millennia, wind blasted and sun baked to artfully sculpted curls of bare wood. Sometimes only one or two branches maintain green needles, but these photosynthesize enough to keep the tree alive. With a tenuous but determined grip on rocky soil, some trees have been clinging to life by the thinnest of threads for centuries. Others have been dead for 2,000 years, but because of the desert-like conditions, their remains still stand. The ultimate bonsai, one bristlecone three inches thick sprouted seven centuries ago.

To me, Joshua Tree National Park is the ultimate California desert. Bulbous rocks accent an undulant landscape; pinnacles and blockhouses of granitic rock rise up out of nowhere. With the stiff, dagger-like leaves of the yucca family, Joshua trees grope for the sky. Though they reach only thirty feet at most, they show a valiant effort to be trees where nothing else comes close.

More than half a million acres in Joshua Tree National Park are safeguarded from development, and more wilderness is protected throughout the desert than in any other region of California. In 1994 the California Desert Protection Act designated 7.6 million acres in all, almost half of it in Death Valley.

Yet the abuses of the desert often seem to dominate, the damages so unbuffered, so raw to the sun and the eye. A spirit of lawlessness has prevailed in backroad areas where miners scrape for minerals that may never be found, where trail bikes and off-road vehicles rip into the soil and crush whatever lies in their paths. A few interstate highways ribbon out in straight lines, and heavy traffic thunders through, Las Vegas to LA, Yuma to San Diego. Sprawl leapfrogs into the emptiness, and from an airplane, new grids of houses and roads look more like a circuit board than an ecosystem. Anywhere within a two-hour commute, the desert is being gobbled up by growth, its hostility to human life well-masked in the age of cheap gasoline and air conditioning.

In the desert, an ethic of land protection took hold much later than in the mountains, along the seashore, and through the forests.

But here in California, activists in love with drylands have tried to catch up. The largest single wilderness proposal in the state includes much of the White Mountains. Additions would be made to Death Valley, Joshua Tree, and a dozen other areas already designated as wilderness. The proposals would help to link now-isolated refuges— a requirement for wildlife such as the rare desert tortoise.

For a final look at the California desert, I went to the Carrizo Basin—an intriguing landscape where additional acreage is proposed for wilderness protection only a few miles from the Mexican border. I wandered through the gullies by day, the spare rays of winter sun hardly touching the ground in rocky canyons. Yet a balminess swept across the land and made me glad to be there while the depths of winter held some other parts of California in a tight grip.

The day rushed by too quickly, and then the nighttime desert enveloped me in its huge embrace. Yet even in the dark, the land held me in its thrall of contrasts. What had been hot was now cold; what had been incandescent in sunny glare was now colorless and shadowy with a tantalizing feel of the unknown, one mystery at each footstep, another at each fingertip. I had a haunting feeling of emptiness, but in fact I knew that the place was full—full of rock and soil, of cacti and ocotillo, of scorpions and ringtails, of bats eating insects I couldn't hear or see.

I had traveled the length of California, from north to south, and while night overtook me and I couldn't possibly imagine all that lay in the darkness at my side, my journey through California had nearly come to an end. With visions of all the land I had seen from Shasta's twilight glow to the sunrise I now awaited near Carrizo Gorge, I knew that the wildness of California brought us life in some ways that we might photograph and describe but in other ways we might never even imagine.

Early morning light reveals layers of ancient sediment on Manly Beacon in Death Valley, seen from Zabriskie Point.
PHOTOGRAPH BY TERRY DONNELLY

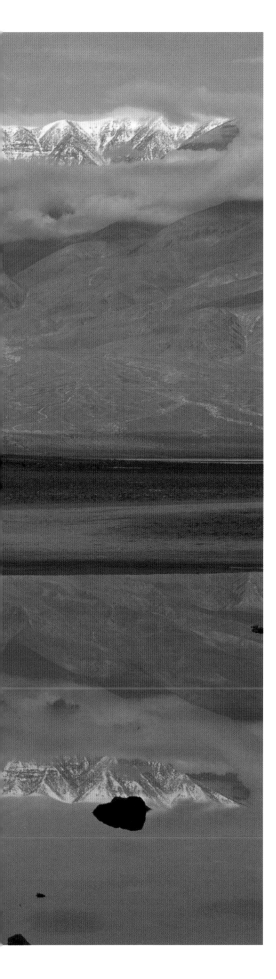

LEFT:
With stark vertical relief, the Panamint Mountains rise up to catch winter snowstorms, which later yield precious moisture to the desert below in Death Valley.
PHOTOGRAPH BY TERRY DONNELLY

ABOVE:
With the moisture of springtime rainstorms, whole fields of desert gold wildflowers appear in Death Valley.
PHOTOGRAPH BY TERRY DONNELLY

RIGHT:
Iron oxides, magnesium, and mica color the hills at
Artist's Palette in Death Valley National Park.
PHOTOGRAPH BY MARY LIZ AUSTIN

BELOW:
California ephedra and sage gain nominal sustenance in a
harsh landscape at Death Valley's Aguereberry Point.
PHOTOGRAPH BY TERRY DONNELLY

FACING PAGE:
At rare times when the desert playa is wet and slick,
the wind blows this rock slowly across the ground
in Death Valley.
PHOTOGRAPH BY TERRY DONNELLY

The White Mountains, with the largest unprotected wilderness in California, rise from the desert near Westgard Pass.

PHOTOGRAPH BY TIM PALMER

Joshua trees and granite boulders are plentiful at Joshua Tree National Park; like Death Valley, protection of this area was upgraded by the California Desert Protection Act of 1994.

PHOTOGRAPH BY TERRY DONNELLY

LEFT:
These bristlecone pines—among the oldest trees in the world—have been growing on the slopes of the White Mountains for thousands of years.
PHOTOGRAPH BY TIM PALMER

BELOW:
Catching the attention of pollinating insects, the claret cup cactus is unmatched for color in the Mojave Desert.
PHOTOGRAPH BY TERRY DONNELLY

RIGHT:
Sunset warms rough, crystalline
surfaces of quartz monzonite in
Joshua Tree National Park.
PHOTOGRAPH BY TERRY DONNELLY

ABOVE:
A favorite winter retreat of rock climbers, Joshua Tree National Park features intricate
geologic formations such as Arch Rock.
PHOTOGRAPH BY TERRY DONNELLY

RIGHT:
Jumbo Rocks in Joshua Tree are roughened, cracked, and fractured by the timeless erosion of wind
and water, by the freezing and thawing of moisture, and by frequent earthquakes.
PHOTOGRAPH BY TERRY DONNELLY

RIGHT:
California fan palms mark the site of the
17 Palm Oasis, with the Santa Rosa
Mountains rising behind.
PHOTOGRAPH BY TERRY DONNELLY

BELOW:
A garden of beavertail cactus, century plant,
brittlebush, and cholla cactus flourish in
Plum Canyon, part of Anza-Borrego
Desert State Park.
PHOTOGRAPH BY TERRY DONNELLY

Erosion from winter rainstorms has sculpted the Borrego Badlands.
PHOTOGRAPH BY TERRY DONNELLY

FAR LEFT:
Brittlebush matures in springtime
with the San Ysidro Mountains and
Indian Head Peak in the background.
PHOTOGRAPH BY TERRY DONNELLY

LEFT:
Barrel cactus blooms in
Anza-Borrego Desert State Park.
PHOTOGRAPH BY TERRY DONNELLY

Wet winters lead to colorful spring-
times in the desert; brittlebush persists
amid rocks in Anza-Borrego.
PHOTOGRAPH BY TERRY DONNELLY

A little-known wilderness, the Mecca Hills lie northeast of the Salton Sea.
PHOTOGRAPH BY TIM PALMER

Ocotillo blooms in the Carrizo Basin. Distant headwaters in the In-ko-pah Mountains are
proposed for wilderness protection.
PHOTOGRAPH BY TIM PALMER

CHAPTER 8

THE FATE OF THE
GOLDEN LAND

What will happen to California?
It has been a wellspring of life and hope for people since the first Americans came as hunters and gatherers from the north, for later arrivals who trekked across Donner Pass at great hazard, for masses of newcomers who journeyed here by railroad or highways, and now for greater numbers than ever—people who come by plane or who cross the border by car or van or on foot, some even arriving through hand-dug tunnels to evade the border patrol. In recent years, far more people have come to California than ever did in the past.

Ages before anybody came, California had been the home and habitat to its native plants and animals—one of the most remarkably diverse collections of flora and fauna known on earth—5,800 kinds of plants and 800 species of wildlife. The remains of that richness stay with us today, though 20 percent of those species are in jeopardy— one in five. Biologists say the main reason is habitat loss; in other words, damage to the land and the rivers. In the past two decades, more than 675,000 acres of wildlands have been degraded—5,800 acres per day. This doesn't count the paving of farmland or the conversion of slightly developed rural open space to suburbia.

California has served the nation by yielding raw resources, everything from gold to old-growth redwood. It has been an economic powerhouse and an undisputed leader in innovative thought and creativity. But California has also inspired people to take care of the land and to preserve something of value for the future, something that can nourish the lives, minds, and spirits of generations unborn. This indispensable role began with John Muir's dedication to save the finest wildness in California. He worked for the establishment of Sequoia and Yosemite National Parks, and wrote, "Thousands of tired, nerve-shaken, over-civilized people are beginning to find out that going to the mountains is going home, that wilderness is a necessity and that mountain parks and reservations are useful not only as fountains of timber and irrigating rivers, but as fountains of life." A century later, in 2002, editors of the *Los Angeles Times* agreed: "Wilderness," they wrote, "can be a perishable thing, succumbing to the bite of the chainsaw, the ruts of the all-terrain vehicle and the seemingly inevitable crush of development. As California's population soars toward 50 million, our remaining wild lands become more precious."

Wildness in nature gives us an alternative beyond the suburbs and the malls, beyond the media frenzy promoting consumerism and beyond the gridlock of smogging vehicles. The wind pulsing in the trees, the foam bubbling up in the rapids, the snow piling deep on whitebark pines and the rain soaking to the roots of the redwoods— these are the heartbeats of life, as important to our spirits as they are to our survival. Wild land possesses this life force in an abundance hardly imagined in our tamed cities and suburbs.

Aspens flame in yellow and orange in Lundy Canyon, on the eastern side of the Sierra.
PHOTOGRAPH BY TERRY DONNELLY

John Muir felt a deeply personal, practical, and spiritual connection to the land, and now, a century after his celebration of beauty, we celebrate it as well. But we also face the question, What will happen to California? In a rapidly changing world, what will be the fate of good land, of nature, of wildness?

In this book, Terry, Mary, and I have shown you pictures from some of our favorite places in California. What will happen to these and to hundreds of other enclaves of wildness? Many are less known than the ones we have photographed but no less important. As a society, we now have a strong heritage of safeguarding parks such as Yosemite and Lassen, the headlands of Marin and Big Sur, and the summits of Whitney and San Gorgonio. But what will happen to the Owens River's source at San Joaquin Ridge where ski lifts are proposed, to San Onofre State Beach where a toll road could be built, to the Mojave at Fort Irwin where a military base could expand into the untracked desert, to Orleans Mountain in the Trinity Alps where old-growth forests could be cut, and to the Gaviota Coast west of Santa Barbara, prime for trophy homes? What future awaits the Klamath River?

Most fundamental among all the trends—the one phenomenon that causes so many others—is that California's population is growing by leaps and bounds. A population of 37 million in 2004 is expected to double in thirty-seven years. Imagine twice the houses, twice the traffic, twice the sprawl, twice the noise and air pollution, and twice the demand for water, jails, and landfills. In only half a lifetime! A new city the size of Los Angeles, every decade! Some human demands may actually more than double. Houses, in fact, have gotten bigger. People drive more, and many of their vehicles use more gas per mile than they did a decade ago. Americans consume twice as much of everything, per capita, as they did in 1950. The population has doubled since then. Now it will double again, and yet again if the trend is not changed.

The effects of predicted population growth will be felt in shock waves through every natural, social, and economic system, from farms to preschools, from depleted commercial fisheries to national parks where "no vacancy" signs go up. More water will be taken from our rivers. More fertile soils will be paved over; the current annual rate of farmland loss is 100,000 acres and climbing, most of it for housing.

No matter how much we try, California cannot accommodate such increased population without a massive disruption of natural systems, without whole clusters of species dropping off the cliff to extinction, without malfunctions in the very workings of nature that make life possible. To combat global warming, for example, is an enormous challenge with the population we already have. Atmospheric scientists say we need to reduce our use of fossil fuels signifi-

cantly. Instead, we use more and more. To address this problem with double the current population seems an utterly futile task.

Beyond the availability of food and water, beyond all the depleted commodities, beyond the overstressed essentials of nature, and beyond the loss of amenities people value so highly, individual freedoms, public safety, and education will all face breakdowns in the culture of unlimited growth. Affecting every person, the quality of life—the California way of life—will be undermined and lost unless we can stabilize our population and consumption levels.

People know they need food and water, but many think they can live without untamed nature. They try to do it all the time in big cities, in sprawling suburbs, in Japan, in Bangladesh. This book is about wildness, so one can't help but ask the question, What difference does wildness make?

For one thing, the loss of wildness means we would see far fewer of the types of scenes shown on every page of this book. This colorful volume could become little more than a historical document of the way life once was in California, never to be visited again. Places as revered as Yosemite might be saved in some nominal and isolated way, but if we lose these wild scenes in less-protected reserves and in connecting landscapes between the parks, we will lose habitat on a massive scale and thereby face the widespread extinction of wild creatures.

Without wildness we would lose the free work that nature does in maintaining its systems of life and in delivering clean air, plentiful water, and even insects that pollinate crops on farms. Beyond all that, we'd lose the timeless record of our human heritage. Our hearts would never again be fulfilled by places that now allow us to escape the clutter of sprawl, to celebrate nature, to appreciate healthy air, good land, and refreshing water.

Even if we succeed in curbing population growth, as we must eventually do, the momentum of past growth alone means a rising population for some years to come. In many respects, the effects of this growth—everything from sprawl to global warming—defy workable solutions. But one important thing can be done, and it can be done with relative ease: the very finest of the remaining wildlands can still be saved.

Here's the current situation in plain numbers. California has 100 million acres in all. About half is publicly owned, mostly by the federal government, meaning we, the taxpayers. However, logging, mining, and damming degrade much of the federal acreage. About 14 million acres are designated as wilderness—congressional status designed to protect "undeveloped federal land retaining its primeval character and influence, without permanent improvements or human habitation." Additionally, the state manages 1 million acres as wildlands. But here's the most important number: 7 million acres of federally owned wilderness remain in California but are *not* protected. This land could be logged, mined, roaded, dammed, or developed unless it's set aside by Congress.

The California Wild Heritage Campaign proposes that Congress safeguard one-third of this unprotected, wild acreage. A project of the California Wilderness Coalition, Friends of the River, The Wilderness Society, Sierra Club, and hundreds of sponsoring groups statewide, the campaign in 2004 proposed to designate 2.5 million acres as wilderness and to name twenty-two new wild and scenic rivers, giving them special status that bans dams and harmful activities by the federal government along the selected streams.

To start this grand endeavor, 57,000 acres of national forest land at the central coast were added to the National Wilderness Preservation System in 2002 in a bill sponsored by congressman Sam Farr. The next year, representative Mike Thompson sponsored a bill to protect 300,000 acres in northern California. Senator Barbara Boxer meanwhile introduced the California Wild Heritage Act to protect eighty-one wilderness sites along with the twenty-two rivers. Announcing her proposal, she said, "History books written about California always comment on the natural beauty of the state because our natural resources have always been one of the things that make California unique. But that beauty must not be taken for granted." While the tenor of national politics prevented the bill from moving, the senator and thousands of supporters pledged themselves for the long haul.

Scarcity is the motivating force behind all this work. Where wildness dominated only 150 years ago, we've converted more than three-quarters of California into something it was not. The wilderness advocates strive for a modest goal: to leave another 2.5 percent of California available for recreation, for wildlife, for spiritual uplift, for scientific use, for hunting, and for fishing, but not for clear-cuts, gravel pits, and dams. Nobody lives on this federal land. It's already owned by the taxpayers. Most of it has relatively little economic value for commodity production or development. Among Californians polled, 72 percent supported additional protection of wilderness and wild rivers.

While the California Wild Heritage Campaign deals only with federal land, a strong case can be made to protect other wild land in California as well. Indeed, the most critical spaces for wildlife are often the more temperate and productive lowlands, and many of the areas most needed for people's recreational use are close to home.

With an eye on these needs, a collaboration of leading corporate, environmental, and public policy leaders called the California Environmental Dialogue estimated that 5.4 million acres of land statewide need to be protected to provide for recreation, agriculture, habitat, wetlands, and open space. Much of this land had to be ac-

quired from private owners at a cost of $12.3 billion in 1999. Though a formidable sum to a state operating in deficit, this is less than one-seventh the amount the U.S. Congress approved for supplemental spending in Iraq in 2004 alone. Many people believe that land protection is something we can afford.

Setting aside wildness today means nothing less than safeguarding a foundation upon which people can restore functioning ecosystems and the balance of nature—something we cannot live without.

In one sense, the land is like ourselves: part is cultured and tame if not completely subdued and separated from the earth's creative forces. But part is *wild*. I think this is the nature of the human spirit. It has always been and always will be. But while the wildness in human nature remains, and while the need for wildness goes undiminished and actually increases as the population grows, the wildness of the land is being lost. Now, only a small amount is left. A balance will be struck only if people act and support others who are acting on behalf of the generations to come.

To complete this tour of wildness in California, I traveled not to another mountain peak, as I had done at Mount Shasta and Whitney and elsewhere in order to see the big view, but to a lower landscape, only twenty miles from the ocean, in the southern end of the state. West of the sprawling new city of Temecula, The Nature Conservancy, Riverside County Regional Park and Open-Space District, and other agencies have worked together to create the Santa Rosa Plateau Ecological Reserve, purchasing more than 8,000 acres from owners who otherwise would have developed the land. A savanna of grass and oak woodlands rolls out in hillsides and valleys, home to a host of wildlife, to rare plants, and to the statuesque Engelmann oak, which grows here in abundance but is found almost nowhere else. Low in elevation and near the Pacific, the countryside supports life in ways that other land does not; the mix of prairie, forest, chaparral, and vernal wetlands create a fascinating combination.

When I visited in February, the long-awaited winter storms had finally come, and within the life-giving cycle of drizzle, shower, and downpour, occasionally interspersed with a few rays of sunshine, I packed up my camera bag and walked the trails of the preserve, quickly winding back beyond the roads and into a world apart. I was accustomed to finding wildness in the more severe landscapes of high country, mountainside, desert, and canyon, but here it lay in grassy swales that curved easily on the land and in groves that seemed to have been created just for the nourishment of life. The scenes here reminded me that all of California, and not just the most remote and extreme samples of this remarkable place, was once wild.

With branches contorted by the ages, coast live oaks shaded the valleys, and on the hillsides the Engelmann oaks still grew into great domes overhead, the leaves tough and leathery, many of them lasting through the winter. Sycamores lined small streambeds where water ran again with the precious runoff delivered by back-to-back storms that pummeled me on some of my walks.

Trails also took me to spacious ridgelines where the savanna lay like a softly painted scene. Farther away, the chaparral darkened slopes of the Santa Ana foothills, which wrinkled down toward the sea. The summits of other mountain ranges lay beneath the overcast, or were partly revealed between wisps of cloud, or lay completely hidden by vapor that thickened as the elevation increased inland. One time, however, a window opened to high country far eastward. The broad-topped summit of Mount San Jacinto, 10,805 feet above sea level, towered briefly above the storm. Lower, but still impressive, Mount Palomar rose to the southeast, and close at hand, the Santa Ana Mountains piled up in folds that stretched northeast to the Los Angeles urban area and also west, where they became the wilds of the San Mateo Canyon Wilderness. The Nature Conservancy and other groups were trying to protect additional land that would reconnect the Santa Rosa Reserve with that great low-elevation wilderness where the Santa Ana Mountains ramp down to the coast.

Although broad, natural corridors linking these and other ranges were usurped long ago, the valleys brimming with development now lay hidden from me, and so the wildness that I saw seemed continuous, just as it once truly was. And in that view was the hope: some wildness remains in thin refuges even down in the lowlands, at the borders of our towns, and at the edges of our backyards.

Standing there in the cool wind, I imagined the corridors of floodplains and the fingers of ridgelines reaching out like rivers of life from my panoramic outpost to the Pacific, to Mexico, to the desert, to the Sierra, and even to the far north—a wildness traceable, if one still looks hard enough, the whole way back to Shasta.

I felt the elusive, mysterious, warmly satisfying sense of being personally connected to all these extraordinary places—to being connected to something greater than myself. The wildness of California is all so beautiful, all so essential as the underpinning of life, so ancient in its elemental imperatives, yet so modern in its appeal.

Thinking of the precious years I have remaining, and thinking of the people who will come this way long after me, even a century or two from now, I hoped that the finest of all I had seen would remain forever wild.

RIGHT:
Zaca Peak rises behind foothills
of valley oaks and grasslands
in early spring.
PHOTOGRAPH BY TIM PALMER

FACING PAGE:
Among the largest of the Sequoias,
this great tree reaches skyward in
the Grant Grove of Sequoia
National Park.
PHOTOGRAPH BY TIM PALMER

The summit of Sanger Peak offers views to ridges and valleys of the Siskiyou Mountains, which harbor the richest diversity of conifer species in the world.
PHOTOGRAPH BY TIM PALMER

Earthquakes have rearranged the geology of the Pacific coast in complex ways, as seen here at Pfeiffer Beach on the Big Sur Coast.
Photograph by Tim Palmer

Fresh snow clings to volcanic rocks along the Middle Fork of the Stanislaus River, upstream from the Clark Fork confluence.
PHOTOGRAPH BY TIM PALMER

At Nevada Falls the Merced River plummets over granite cliffs and splays onto bedrock below.

PHOTOGRAPH BY TIM PALMER

The eastern Sierra towers above volcanic rocks near Taboose Creek.

PHOTOGRAPH BY TIM PALMER

The incomparable red of a desert sunset flames behind a Joshua tree in the Mojave Desert.
PHOTOGRAPH BY TIM PALMER

CONSERVATION ORGANIZATIONS

Audubon California
87 North Raymond Avenue, Suite 700
Pasadena, CA, 91103
(626) 564-1300
www.audubon-ca.org

California Native Plant Society
2707 K Street
Sacramento, CA 95816
(916) 447-2677
www.cnps.org

California Oak Foundation
1212 Broadway, Suite 810
Oakland, CA 94612
(510) 763-0282
www.californiaoaks.org

California Wilderness Coalition
2655 Portage Bay East
Davis, CA 95616
(805) 963-1622
www.calwild.org

California Wild Heritage Campaign
(916) 442-3155
www.californiawild.org

Friends of the River
915 20th Street
Sacramento, CA 95814
(916) 442-3155
www.friendsoftheriver.org

Greenbelt Alliance
631 Howard Street, Suite 510
San Francisco, CA 94105
(415) 543-6771
www.greenbelt.org

Keep Sespe Wild Committee
P.O. Box 715
Ojai, CA 93024
(805) 921-0618
www.sespewild.org

League to Save Lake Tahoe
955 Emerald Bay Road
South Lake Tahoe, CA 96150
(530) 541-5388
www.keeptahoeblue.org

The Nature Conservancy
201 Mission Street, 4th floor
San Francisco, CA 94105
(415) 777-0487
www.tnccalifornia.org

Northcoast Environmental Center
575 H Street
Arcata, CA 95521
(707) 822-6918
www.necandeconews.to

Planning and Conservation League
926 J Street, #612
Sacramento, CA 95814
(916) 444-8726
www.pcl.org

Sequoia Wild Heritage Project
P.O. Box 3543
Visalia, CA 93278
(559) 739-8527
www.californiawild.org

Sierra Club (with groups statewide)
827 Broadway, Suite 310
Oakland, CA 94607
(510) 622-0290
www.sierraclub.org

Sierra Nevada Alliance
P.O. Box 7989
South Lake Tahoe, CA 96158
(530) 542-4546
www.sierranevadaalliance.org

Tree People
12601 Mulholland Drive
Beverly Hills, CA 90210
(818) 753-4600
www.treepeople.org

Ventana Wilderness Alliance
P.O. Box 506
Santa Cruz, CA 95061
(831) 423-3191
www.ventanawild.org

The Wilderness Society
P. O. Box 29241
San Francisco, CA 94129
(415) 561-6641
www.wilderness.org

BIBLIOGRAPHY

Bakker, Elna. *An Island Called California: An Ecological Introduction to its Natural Communities.* Berkeley: University of California Press, 1971.

Barbour, Michael, and Bruce Pavlik, Frank Drysdale, and Susan Lindstrom. *California's Changing Landscapes: Diversity and Conservation of California Vegetation.* Sacramento: California Native Plant Society, 1993.

California Environmental Dialogue. *Land Conservation in California.* Sacramento: California Environmental Dialogue, 1999, available from the Planning and Conservation League.

California Nature Conservancy. *Sliding Toward Extinction: the State of California's Natural Heritage, 1987.* San Francisco: California Nature Conservancy, 1987.

California Oak Foundation. *California Oaks: Their Status and Conservation Needs.* Sacramento: California Oak Foundation, 1980.

California Wilderness Coalition. *California's Last Wild Places.* Davis: California Wilderness Coalition, 2001.

California Wilderness Coalition. *California's 10 Most Threatened Wild Places.* Davis: California Wilderness Coalition, 2003.

California Wilderness Coalition. *Briefing Papers for California Wild Heritage Campaign.* Davis: California Wilderness Coalition, 2003.

Centers for Water and Wildlands Resources. *Status of the Sierra Nevada—Sierra Nevada Ecosystem Project.* Davis: University of California, 1996.

Davis, Mike. *Ecology of Fear: Los Angeles and the Imagination of Disaster.* New York: Henry Holt, 1998.

Duane, Timothy P. *Shaping the Sierra: Nature, Culture, and Conflict in the Changing West.* Berkeley: University of California Press, 1998.

Evens, Jules G. *The Natural History of the Point Reyes Peninsula.* Point Reyes: Point Reyes National Seashore Association, 1993.

Fradkin, Philip L. *The Seven States of California.* New York: Henry Holt, 1995.

Friends of the River. *National Wild and Scenic Rivers in California: A Status Report.* Sacramento: Friends of the River, 1998.

Friends of the River. *Potential Wild and Scenic Rivers in California: A Statewide Inventory.* Sacramento: Friends of the River, 2001.

Harden, Deborah R. *California Geology.* Upper Saddle River, NJ: Prentice Hall, 1998.

Henson, Paul, and Donald J. Usner. *The Natural History of Big Sur.* Berkeley: University of California Press, 1993.

Hundley, Norris Jr. *The Great Thirst: Californians and Water, 1770s–1990s.* Berkeley: University of California Press, 1992.

Jensen, Deborah B., Margaret S. Tom, and John Harte. *In Our Hands: A Strategy for Conserving California's Biological Diversity.* Berkeley: University of California Press, 1993.

Johnston, Verna R. *California Forests and Woodlands: A Natural History.* Berkeley: University of California Press, 1994.

Knudson, Tom. "The Sierra in Peril," *Sacramento Bee*, special report, June 13, 1991.

Lufkin, Alan, ed. *California's Salmon and Steelhead.* Berkeley: University of California Press, 1991.

Mann, Eric. *L.A.'s Lethal Air: New Strategies for Policy, Organizing, and Action.* Los Angeles: Labor/Community Strategy Center, 1991.

McPhee, John. *Assembling California.* New York: Farrar, Straus and Giroux, 1993.

Mount, Jeffrey F. *California Rivers and Streams: the Conflict Between Fluvial Process and Land Use.* Berkeley: University of California Press, 1995.

Muir, John. *The Mountains of California.* New York: Doubleday, 1961.

Noss, Reed F. *The Redwood Forest.* Washington, D.C.: Island Press, 2000.

Palmer, Tim, ed. *California's Threatened Environment.* Washington, D.C.: Island Press, 1993.

Palmer, Tim. *Pacific High: Adventures in the Coast Ranges from Baja to Alaska.* Washington, D.C.: Island Press, 2002.

Palmer, Tim. *The Sierra Nevada: A Mountain Journey.* Washington, D.C.: Island Press, 1988.

Palmer Tim, and William Neill. *Yosemite: The Promise of Wildness.* El Portal: The Yosemite Association, 1994.

Rose, Gene. *San Joaquin: A River Betrayed.* Fresno: Linrose Publishing Co., 1992

Schoenherr, Allan A. *A Natural History of California.* Berkeley: University of California Press, 1992.

Schrag, Peter. *Paradise Lost: California's Experience, America's Future.* Berkeley: University of California Press, 1999.

Storer, Tracy I. and Robert L. Usinger. *Sierra Nevada Natural History.* Berkeley: University of California Press, 1963.

Strong, Douglas H. *Tahoe: An Environmental History.* Lincoln: University of Nebraska Press, 1984.

Thelander, Carl, ed. *Life on the Edge: A Guide to California's Endangered Natural Resources.* Santa Cruz: BioSystems Books, 1994.

Wuerthner, George. *California's Wilderness Areas: Volume 1, Mountains and Coastal Ranges.* Englewood, CO: Westcliffe, 1997.

Wuerthner, George. *California's Wilderness Areas: Volume 2, The Deserts.* Englewood, CO: Westcliffe, 1999.

Index

ABOUT THE AUTHOR
AND PHOTOGRAPHERS

Tim Palmer is the author of fifteen books, including *The Sierra Nevada: A Mountain Journey*, *California's Threatened Environment*, and *America by Rivers*. He wrote the text for *Yosemite: the Promise of Wildness*, which won the Director's Award for the best book about a national park in 1997. His 2002 travel book, *Pacific High: Adventures in the Coast Ranges from Baja to Alaska*, was a finalist for the Ben Franklin Book Award, and *The Heart of America: Our Landscape, Our Future* won the Independent Book Publishers Award. He also wrote the text for *Oregon: Preserving the Beauty and Spirit of the Land*, published by Voyageur Press in 2003.

Tim first came to California in 1967 as a hitch-hiker and fell in love with Yosemite, the Sierra Nevada, the Pacific, and the other mountains and wildlands of this state. In 1980 he moved to California full-time to write a book about the Stanislaus River and Friends of the River's effort to save it. Since then he has been a resident of the state much of the time and has traveled extensively on foot, by canoe and whitewater raft, on skis, by mountain bike, and in his well-equipped van. He never tires of learning about California and photographing its beauty and nature.

For more than eighteen years, photographers Terry Donnelly and Mary Liz Austin have traveled extensively throughout North America, Europe, and the South Pacific photographing the wonders of nature, travel destinations, national parks, and the American countryside. Their work has been widely published in numerous books, periodicals, and calendars. Their previous books include *Heaven on Earth*; *Seattle*; *Washington: the Spirit of the Land*; *Oregon: Preserving the Spirit and Beauty of Our Land*; and, most recently, *Wild Seattle*. Donnelly and Austin make their home on Vashon Island, Washington.